Entrepreneurship in F

Ramo Palalić • Léo-Paul Dana • Veland Ramadani
Editors

Entrepreneurship in Former Yugoslavia

Diversity, Institutional Constraints and
Prospects

 Springer

Editors
Ramo Palalić
International University of Sarajevo
Sarajevo, Bosnia and Herzegovina

Léo-Paul Dana
Montpellier Business School
Montpellier, France

Veland Ramadani
Faculty of Business and Economics
South-East European University
Tetovo, Macedonia

ISBN 978-3-319-77633-0   ISBN 978-3-319-77634-7   (eBook)
https://doi.org/10.1007/978-3-319-77634-7

Library of Congress Control Number: 2018940667

Printed on acid-free paper

This Springer imprint is published by the registered company Springer International Publishing AG part of Springer Nature.
The registered company address is: Gewerbestrasse 11, 6330 Cham, Switzerland

To my beloved wife Sadina and daughter Isra
Ramo Palalić

*In memory of my parents, from whom I
learned to respect and love the Balkans*
Léo-Paul Dana

*To my father, Ismet Ramadani—an active
participant in the political movements before,
during, and after the collapse of Yugoslavia*
Veland Ramadani

.

Foreword

Once upon a time there used to be a country called Yugoslavia that existed for less than 75 years. Reflecting on its various nations and history, Yugoslavia was never really a unified country. Shortly after the death of the long-living iconic national leader Josip Broz Tito in 1980, the disintegration of the country started. Many remember the clash that ended Yugoslavia causing hundreds of thousands of casualties and a million to seek refuge in the 1990s. While the physical war ended, the pressure still exists mainly in Bosnia and Herzegovina and in Kosovo.

For understanding the present situation in any former Yugoslavian country, someone should know its history. In particular, entrepreneurship has its roots in the specific Yugoslavian model of self-managed socialism with partially decentralized decision making. While this experience, similar to other socialist reform movements, was based on the denial of private property and entrepreneurship, it still allowed some limited artisans, craftsmanship, and agricultural farming. Finally, this unique model together with other socialist reform movements proved to be unsuccessful mainly because of the lack of operational demand and supply-oriented market signals and the associated distorted incentive structure. This heritage still has an impact on many former Yugoslavian successor states.

For entrepreneurship development a country needs two things: enterprising individuals and favorable environment. Yugoslavia's partial transition to the market economy started in 1988 by allowing private business start-ups. Shortly, hundreds of thousands of new establishments appeared all over the country. However, if someone thinks about entrepreneurship as creating the next Google, Spotify, Uber, or Xiaomi, he or she should look elsewhere, not in the former Yugoslavian countries. Small, family businesses, shops, artisans, and tourist-related ventures dominate most in these countries struggling to survive and grow. While many studies in this book write about the low level of business start-up activity in many countries, the real problem is the lack of high growth, innovative export-oriented firms, and local heroes making a fortune out of individual efforts and not state support.

Institutional reforms proceeded slowly and unevenly in the successor Yugoslavian states limiting the development of the private business sector in many cases.

According to the World Bank *Doing Business 2017* report, former Yugoslavian countries rank between 11th (Macedonia) and 86th (Bosnia and Herzegovina). Starting and growing a new business is challenging, and future entrepreneurs should also deal with high corruption. Small local markets and declining population—except Kosovo—also limit business growth.

Privatization was also not a success story and state ownership is still playing a dominant role in all countries. While another neighboring transition country, Hungary, has been blamed for selling the "family jewelry" to foreigners, former Yugoslavian countries occupy the other extreme position. According to the World Bank Foreign Direct Investment (FDI) data from 2016, Hungary alone has around ten times more FDI than all the seven former Yugoslavian successors together. The lack of foreign businesses and multinationals prevents these countries to integrate better in the world economy by subcontracting and to capitalize on technology transfers and management practices.

According to the famous philosopher, novelist, and poet, George Santayana: "Those who cannot remember the past are condemned to repeat it." So I recommend this book to all of you who want to learn from the past and would like to know how to build a new future.

Faculty of Business and Economics,   László Szerb
Head of Department of Quantitative
Management, University of Pécs, Pécs,
Hungary

Contents

Editors and Contributors

About the Editors

Ramo Palalić is an assistant professor in the Management Program, Faculty of Business and Administration, International University of Sarajevo, Sarajevo, Bosnia and Herzegovina. His research interests are entrepreneurship, leadership, marketing, and management. He teaches at both undergraduate and postgraduate levels in the above areas. Apart from this, he is actively involved in business projects in the areas of entrepreneurial leadership and marketing management, in private and public organizations. He has authored and coauthored several articles in reputable international journals. Currently, he is serving a few journals as reviewer/editor board member.

Léo-Paul Dana earned BA and MBA degrees at McGill University and a PhD from HEC-Montreal. He is professor of entrepreneurship at Montpellier Business School and a member of the Entrepreneurship & Innovation chair of LabEx Entrepreneurship (University of Montpellier, France). He formerly served as visiting professor of entrepreneurship at INSEAD and deputy director of the International Business MBA Programme at Nanyang Business School. He has published extensively in a variety of leading journals including the *British Food Journal, Cornell Quarterly, Entrepreneurship and Regional Development, Entrepreneurship: Theory and Practice, Journal of Small Business Management, Journal of World Business,* and *Small Business Economics*. His research interests focus on cultural issues, including the internationalization of entrepreneurship.

 **Veland Ramadani** is an associate professor at South-East European University, Republic of Macedonia, where he teaches both undergraduate and postgraduate courses in entrepreneurship and small business management. His research interests include entrepreneurship, small business management, family businesses, and venture capital investments. He authored or coauthored around eighty research articles and seventeen books. Dr. Ramadani is an associate editor of *International Journal of Entrepreneurship and Small Business (IJESB)*. Dr. Ramadani received the Award for Excellence 2016—Outstanding Paper by Emerald Group Publishing (*Journal of Enterprising Communities: People and Places in the Global Economy*).

Contributors

Mirela Alpeza J.J. Strossmayer University in Osijek, Osijek, Croatia

Bostjan Antoncic University of Ljubljana, Slovenia

Azra Bičo International University of Sarajevo, Sarajevo, Bosnia and Herzegovina

Léo-Paul Dana Montpellier Business School, Montpellier, France

Maja Ivanović Đukić University of Niš, Niš, Serbia

Shqipe Gërguri-Rashiti American College of the Middle-East, Eqaila, Kuwait

Maja Has University of Zagreb, Zagreb, Croatia

Robert D. Hisrich Kent State University, Kent, OH, USA

Besnik A. Krasniqi University of Prishtina "Hasan Prishtina", Republic of Kosovo

Muhamet Mustafa Riinvest College, Prishtina, Republic of Kosovo

Ramo Palalić International University of Sarajevo, Sarajevo, Bosnia and Herzegovina

Laxman Panthi Medical Mutual of Omaha, Omaha, NE, USA

Suncica Oberman Peterka J.J. Strossmayer University in Osijek, Osijek, Croatia

Saša Petković University of Banja Luka, Banja Luka, Bosnia and Herzegovina

Veland Ramadani South-East European University, Tetovo, Macedonia

Vanessa Ratten La Trobe University, Melbourne, Australia

Gadaf Rexhepi South-East European University, Tetovo, Macedonia

Entrepreneurship in Former Yugoslavia: An Introduction

Léo Paul Dana, Ramo Palalić, and Veland Ramadani

Abstract This chapter depicts historical development of former Yugoslavia, from its inception to the dissolution. Details about Yugopluralist models are given, such as milestones, functions, and consequences of its model. Other details related to Yugoslavia's internal and external performance from 1945 to 1989 are discussed.

1 Historical Overview of Yugoslavia

Yugoslavia was consisted of six independent republics and two autonomous provinces. These republics were Slovenia, Croatia, Bosnia and Herzegovina, Serbia, Montenegro, and Macedonia, and Kosovo and Vojvodina were provinces. Although the official language (Serbo-Croatian) was uniform and spoken across former Yugoslavia, all the republics and provinces had a different cultural background (Dana and Ramadani 2015).

Before the Austro-Hungarian Empire, the region of Bosnia and Herzegovina along with Serbia, Macedonia, and Montenegro were constituents of the Ottoman Empire, from 1463 up to 1878. By the Berlin's Congress of 1878, Bosnia and Herzegovina was occupied by the Austro-Hungarian Empire, while Serbia and Montenegro were granted independence. Macedonia remained under the Ottoman Empire. In the twentieth century, a first Yugoslavian model was established by the Kingdom of Serbs, Croats, and Slovenes (Kingdom of SCS), to which later, Montenegro and Macedonia were added (Chater 1930, p. 264)—but prior to that, the 1914 assassination

L. P. Dana
Montpellier Business School, Montpellier, France
e-mail: lp.dana@supco-montpellier.fr; lp.dana@Montpellier-BS.com

R. Palalić (✉)
International University of Sarajevo, Sarajevo, Bosnia and Herzegovina
e-mail: rpalalic@ius.edu.ba

V. Ramadani
South-East European University, Tetovo, Macedonia
e-mail: v.ramadani@seeu.edu.mk

© Springer International Publishing AG, part of Springer Nature 2018   1
R. Palalić et al. (eds.), *Entrepreneurship in Former Yugoslavia*,
https://doi.org/10.1007/978-3-319-77634-7_1

of the Austrian archduke, Franz Ferdinand, resulted in the great War, later renamed World War I (Dana 2010; Ramadani and Dana 2013).

Soon after establishment of the Kingdom of SCS, Aleksandar I was inaugurated as the absolute ruler of the kingdom. This decision did not satisfy the core members of the kingdom; Croats disliked this and felt insulted (Dana 2010). After few years, in 1929, the Kingdom of SCS was renamed Kingdom of Yugoslavia, which in local language means "Land of Southern Slavs" (Chater 1930). The rule of Aleksandar Karadjordjevic ended in 1934 when he was assassinated in Marseilles (Dana 2010).

During World War II, the Kingdom of Yugoslavia tried to respond to the war's challenges. At the time, Josip Broz Tito was a leader of Partisans in freeing the region of Kingdom of Yugoslavia (Dana 2010) from Nazi Germany. At the end of World War II, Tito with his peers established the Federation of Peoples of Yugoslavia, which later was changed into Socialist Federation Republic of Yugoslavia. Due to Tito's contribution to freedom of Yugoslavia, Podgorica was renamed Titograd—today, capital of Montenegro (Dana 2010, p. 43). Later, all constitutive republics and provinces renamed one city or town in honor of Tito, for example: Titovo Velenje (Slovenia), Titova Korenica (Croatia), Titov Drvar (Bosnia and Herzegovina), Titovo užice (Serbia), Titov Veles (Macedonia), Titova Mitrovica (Kosovo), and Titov Vrbas (Vojvodina)".

Soon after World War II, Tito started to make Yugoslavia unaligned with Soviet communism; it was a brave move to be neither aligned with the West nor with the Warsaw bloc. Although, in 1948, Tito was given a serious warning from Soviet Union that he could lead Yugoslavia this way, Tito refused and remained unaligned. Tito has gained a power in this period and began to introduce a very "aggressive foreign policy" towards neighbor countries (Italy, Austria, Bulgaria, Greece, and Albania) to the extent of expansion of the Yugoslavia on these territories (Niebuhr 2017, p. 301). However, in this battle he was not successful as he was also against the Soviet bloc.

In terms of diverse culture in the region of former Yugoslavia, Jordan (1970) observed "Yugoslavs use two alphabets, embrace three religious faiths, speak three main languages and numerous other tongues (p. 592)." As a diverse and pluralistic country, Yugoslavia remained strong until the death of Tito in 1980 (Dana 1994, 2010). Then, the leadership of Yugoslavia was taken over by Serbs in Belgrade, which Slovenia and Croatia resented and slowly paved the way for independence. The independence of these took a decade as it was not easy to implement given that Yugoslavia was based on its brotherhood and unity—in Serbo-Croatian: *bratstvo i jedinstvo*. At the time, other republics (Macedonia, Montenegro, and Bosnia and Herzegovina) were not aware of the independence option, as were Slovenia and Croatia.

2   State of Entrepreneurship in Former Yugoslavia

Under the postwar leadership of Tito, Yugoslavia began to introduce nationalization of the economy. The first nationalized was agriculture while entrepreneurs—or *limited artisans*—were heavily taxed (Dana 2010). Grosvenor (1962, p. 241) noted that number of workers allowed at the time was three, while in 1965 it is increased to five, and ten in 1983 (Dana 2010, p. 44).

Being nonaligned with the Soviet Union, Tito had led Yugoslavia as specific state model so-called self-managing socialism (Dana 2010, p. 44). It was a centralized power, as command economy system (Palalic et al. 2017) in the capital city of Yugoslavia, Belgrade, while development of the country was chained through the municipalities (so-called communes), which were 500 across the whole country (Dana 2010, p. 44).

Entrepreneurship in Yugoslavia was often understood as a negative phenomenon—a product of *greedy capitalism* established on exploitation of others' work (Glas 1998). Although it was not free market in Yugoslavia, in late 1980s, and entrepreneurship was not developed, Yugoslavia's "gross social product (Eastern European version of gross domestic product)" was quite stable (Dana 2010, p. 45).

Such self-managing socialism was quite stable, and the whole industry was circulated across the country. Supply chain was well organized, and outputs were tremendous. Wealthy with natural resources, Tito's Yugoslavia under this system was able to produce and make export to regions other than Europe, like the Middle East, North Africa, South East Asia, and the Gulf region.

During these 1980s, entrepreneurship started to knock on the Yugoslavia's door. The Enterprise Law has recognized private ownership (Dana 2010). However, the business environment was not fertile for entrepreneurship development. The country was in declining stage while each Republics was dreaming of its independence. Such political, socioeconomic chaos impacted the real economy. For instance, the inflation rate in 1989 was recorded as 2700% (The Economist 1990). The Yugopluralist (Dana 1994) model was almost collapsed. Products of such non-working model in post-Tito period produced several noncommunist movements across Slovenia and Croatia (Dana 2010).

Business transactions between Yugoslavia's republics decreased, whereas each of them was looking for a light in the dark night. Such objective constraints led republics to start a trial-state behavior (behaved as states).

The Yugopluralist model was based on pluralism of different cultures contributed by each Yugoslavia's republic. Some of them had been already entrepreneurially oriented compared to others. In this context, Weber (1904–1905) summarized that cultures differ in terms of entrepreneurial conduct and some of them are more inclined than others. Thus, culturally more connected to the Western Europe, Slovenia and Croatia started entrepreneurial spirit across their regions. Although these activities were limited to small "craftsmen, repairmen and eating establishments" (Dana 2010, p. 46), still they were very motivated and believed in their entrepreneurial activities. Glas et al. (2000) noted that Slovenia and Croatia were the

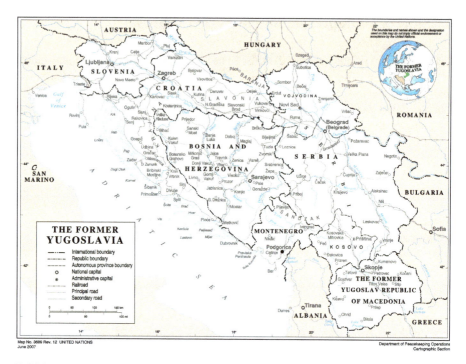

Exhibit 1 The Former Yugoslavia, Map No. 3689 Rev.12, June 2007, Source: United Nations. Available on (http://www.un.org/Depts/Cartographic/map/profile/frmryugo.pdf). Accessed on 19.12.2017

most developed republics in former Yugoslavia. For instance, one-third of Yugoslavia's exports were produced in Slovenia, and 50% of Slovenia's GNP was being taken by the central government for redistribution to less developed republics (Dana 2010, pp. 48–49).

In the last decade of the Yugopluralist model, the "new dinar" (worth 10,000 dinars) was introduced. It was pegged for German mark. The new dinar was controlled by the federal Government so that it could not be converted into other currencies except German mark. This was a response to the hyper-inflation rate in the late 1980s. This period was marked as first steps towards market-driven economy in which Yugoslavia's citizens could make business transactions in Austria and Italy.

Taking into consideration a diverse cultural environment of all six republics (Exhibit 1), as well as weak Federal Government, the entrepreneurial activities could not be distributed equally. This status enabled each Republic government to lead entrepreneurial activities in a way in which its culture prevails. Thus, Slovenia and Croatia were more entrepreneurship development oriented compared to others, and they were implementing market economy with more relaxed taxes for startups and new ventures.

3   Former Yugoslavia After Tito's Era: Political and Economic Context

After Tito's death, it was somehow foreseen challenges of the existence of the Yugopluralist model. Heterogeneity of the Yugoslavia's culture, unequal economic and social development among republics led to collapse of the model. The highest authority (Tito) was no longer in power, and the Federal Government increasingly weakened. The government could not *discipline* those republics that trace their paths toward free-market economy and implement neither Federal Government activities nor support its own republic's economic strategy.

A strong new dinar helped Slovenia and Croatia to establish a good basis for entrepreneurship ecosystem. Another favor that was contributed to implementation of the market-driven economy of these two republics was that in 1990 "Yugoslav parliament's constitutional commission, suggesting that republics should have the right to secede" (Dana 2010, p. 50). Slovenia and Croatia gained independence on June 25, 1991, while others were waiting. Meantime, Serbia and Montenegro continued with communism. Macedonia declared its sovereignty in September 1991 and Bosnia and Herzegovina on October 15, 1991 (Dana 2010, p. 50).

The only republics that wanted to remain in Yugoslavia were Serbia and Montenegro. They formed Federation Republic of Yugoslavia (*Savezna Republika Jugoslavia*) which was under international sanction from 1991 to 1992, due to invading aims over Croatia.

Finally, former Yugoslavia was the first of social countries that accepted reforms toward market-driven economy; however, only two of them implemented. These republics (Slovenia and Croatia) were culturally more oriented toward entrepreneurship due to their similarities to the European cultural values.

Dana (2010) summarized: "Yugopluralist Model, because of the decentralization of policy that it allowed, led to increased regional disparities. For those welcoming entrepreneurship, the ability to express cultural pluralism resulted in economic pluralism. Successful republics resented demands by the federal government to subsidize the less-entrepreneurial republics. While Yugoslavia was among the first socialist countries to welcome reform, only some Yugoslav republics accepted genuine change. Historical and cultural factors appear to be the causal variables. Successful republics resented demands by the federal government to subsidize the less-entrepreneurial republics. The result was war and the demise of the former Federation (pp. 50–51)".

The book aims to describe the history of each country that was part of Yugoslavia, the actual economic environment, entrepreneurship development, promoting activities and measures to increase the entrepreneurial activities, opportunities for new businesses, and foreign entrepreneurs and recommendation for the future. The book consists of nine chapters. Followed by the introduction chapter, seven of them describe each republic of former Yugoslavia, including Kosovo, which declared its independence from Serbia on February 17, 2008. The last chapter (ninth) reviews the current state of economies of all former Yugoslavia's republics, emphasizing their future perspectives regarding the development of the entrepreneurship.

References

Chater, M. (1930). Jugoslavia – ten years after. *National Geographic, 58*(3), 257–309.

Dana, L.-P. (1994). The impact of culture on entrepreneurship, innovation, and change in the Balkans: The Yugopluralist model. *Entrepreneurship, Innovation, and Change, 3*(2), 177–190.

Dana, L.-P. (2010). *When economies change hands: A survey of entrepreneurship in the emerging markets of Europe from the Balkans to the Baltic States*. New York: Routledge.

Dana, L.-P., & Ramadani, V. (Eds.). (2015). *Family business in transition economies*. Cham: Springer.

Glas, M., Drnovšek, M., & Damjan, M. (2000, September 20–22). *Problems faced by new entrepreneurs: Slovenia and Croatia – A comparison*. Paper presented at the 30th European small business seminar, entrepreneurship under difficult circumstances, Gent, Belgium: EFMD Vlerick Leuven Gent Management School.

Glas, M. (1998). Eastern Europe: Slovenia. In A. J. Morrison (Ed.), *Entrepreneurship – An international perspective* (pp. 108–124). Oxford: Heinemann.

Grosvenor, G. M. (1962, February). Yugoslavia's window on the Adriatic. *National Geographic, 121*(2), 219–247.

Niebuhr, R. (2017). Enlarging Yugoslavia: Tito's quest for expansion, 1945–1948. *European History Quarterly, 47*(2), 284–310.

Palalic, R., Ramadani, V., & Dana, L. P. (2017). Entrepreneurship in Bosnia and Herzegovina: Focus on gender. *European Business Review, 29*(4), 476–496.

Ramadani, V., & Dana, L.-P. (2013). The state of entrepreneurship in the Balkans: Evidence from selected countries. In V. Ramadani & R. Schneider (Eds.), *Entrepreneurship in the Balkans* (pp. 217–250). Heidelberg: Springer.

The Economist. (1990, June 23). *Yugoslavia* (p. 103).

Léo-Paul Dana earned BA and MBA degrees at McGill University and a PhD from HEC-Montreal. He is professor of Entrepreneurship at Montpellier Business School and a member of the Entrepreneurship & Innovation chair of LabEx Entrepreneurship (University of Montpellier, France). He formerly served as visiting professor of Entrepreneurship at INSEAD and deputy director of the International Business MBA Programme at Nanyang Business School. He has published extensively in a variety of leading journals including the *British Food Journal, Cornell Quarterly, Entrepreneurship and Regional Development, Entrepreneurship: Theory and Practice, Journal of Small Business Management, Journal of World Business,* and *Small Business Economics.* His research interests focus on cultural issues, including the internationalization of entrepreneurship.

Ramo Palalić is an assistant professor at the Management Program, Faculty of Business and Administration, International University of Sarajevo, Sarajevo, Bosnia and Herzegovina. His research interests are entrepreneurship, leadership, marketing, and management. He teaches at both undergraduate and postgraduate levels in the above areas. Apart from this, he is actively involved in business projects in the areas of entrepreneurial leadership and marketing management and in private and public organizations. He has authored and coauthored several articles in the reputable international journals. Currently, he is serving a few journals as reviewer/editor board member.

Veland Ramadani is an associate professor at South-East European University, Republic of Macedonia, where he teaches both undergraduate and postgraduate courses in entrepreneurship and small business management. His research interests include entrepreneurship, small business management, family businesses, and venture capital investments. He authored or coauthored around 80 research articles and 17 books. Dr. Ramadani is an associate editor of *International Journal of Entrepreneurship and Small Business (IJESB)*. Dr. Ramadani received the Award for Excellence 2015—Outstanding Reviewer by Emerald Group Publishing (*Journal of Enterprising Communities: People and Places in the Global Economy*).

Entrepreneurship in Bosnia and Herzegovina

Ramo Palalić and Azra Bičo

Abstract This chapter depicts a glance picture of Bosnian state of entrepreneurship. It begins with a historical overview and establishment of the state. It describes the challenges that Bosnia has faced as well as its current issues. The current state of entrepreneurship, business environment, and problems of entrepreneurs and small business owners are discussed. The chapter concludes suggestions for further development of entrepreneurship in Bosnia and Herzegovina.

1 Introduction

Bosnia and Herzegovina (B&H) is located on the Balkan Peninsula. It covers an area of 51,197 km^2, and it is bordering Croatia to the north and west, Serbia to the east, Montenegro to the southeast, and the Adriatic Sea to the south with its coastline that has very limited access at the Adriatic Sea of 20 km length. The landscape is mostly hilly and mountainous with almost 50% of landmass composed of thick forest intertwined with fertile river valleys. Flag of Bosnia and Herzegovina is showed in the (Exhibit 1).

Such geography has profoundly influenced country's economic activities during previous Former Yugoslav (FY) economic system, and nowadays during a period of transition to the modern market economy, where the production is mostly relying on and related to the usage of its resources. B&H is rich in terms of natural resources such as minerals and metals among which coal limestone, bauxite, copper, lead, and zinc are dominating. Hence, the economy itself relies heavily on exports of natural resources such as metals and energy. During FY Period, heavy industry was dominating B&H's labor market. B&H's economy was major supplier of raw materials and semi-finished products for processing industries in other Federal republics of Yugoslavia. What Bosnia and Herzegovina can be especially proud of are its water resources, that are abundant and of high quality.

R. Palalić (✉) · A. Bičo
International University of Sarajevo, Sarajevo, Bosnia and Herzegovina
e-mail: rpalalic@ius.edu.ba; abico@ius.edu.ba

© Springer International Publishing AG, part of Springer Nature 2018
R. Palalić et al. (eds.), *Entrepreneurship in Former Yugoslavia*,
https://doi.org/10.1007/978-3-319-77634-7_2

Exhibit 1 Flag of Bosnia and Herzegovina

Exhibit 2 Sarajevo; photo © 2017 Azra Bičo

A former member of Yugoslavia, Bosnia and Herzegovina declared its independence on 1st of March 1992. Following events are deadly attacks by Serb aggressors on B&H's civil society, B&H was confronted with severe humanitarian and social problems in which thousands of people died, and a considerable part of the population seeks for refugees (Ilgün and Coşkun 2009).

The conflict lasted until the Dayton Peace Agreement was signed in Paris in December 1995 between the counterparts. As a result, B&H consists of two entities, The Federation of Bosnia and Herzegovina (FB&H) with 51% of the territory and Sarajevo (Exhibit 2) as its capital. Sarajevo is also the national capital city. Another entity is Republika Srpska (RS) with 49% of the territory, and its capital is Banja Luka. The Federation is further divided into ten autonomous cantons.

Unemployment rate by International Labor Organization is exceptionally high amounting to 32.2% in the year 2016. Reason for it is a process of transition because the private sector is unable to inject workers that are leaving from the public sector or from the major product lines that were shut down after the war. In favor of these figures goes the fact that the majority of Bosnians and Herzegovinians are more likely to be listed as employed than as self-employed. Therefore, self-employment consciousness is still at shallow levels, and it is one of the necessary improvements that need to be made, through the promotion of both active and passive labor market policies; it can positively affect the situation in the economy and decrease these severe unemployment rates.

Under central planning, economic development in Bosnia and Herzegovina was based on state ownership, after independence and civil war; the rebuilding of the economy was left to a private businessman (Dana and Dana 2003). There is a sole initiative from local businessmen as well as from disaspora. However, the local initiative in Bosnia and Herzegovina is hindered by many obstacles like the persistence of lengthy, rigid bureaucratic procedures, corruption, and the inefficiency of the judicial system. All these are not favorable for local businessmen and even for potential foreign investors.

Due to poor general infrastructure, the country is still quite closed when it comes to trading, much improvement is needed, and the highways are not completed, and it is of foremost importance for connections to Europe to access European markets. On the contrary, its location is desirable, and B&H could be a possible bridge between east and west, upon completing needed infrastructural projects. Bosnia and Herzegovina is ideally located, and its proximity to the main European business hubs makes it an attractive business destination. Among its population of 3.8 million, significant number of it are skilled labor force (Bičo and Bajram 2012).

Bosnia and Herzegovina belongs to a group of upper-middle-income countries, and in the year of 2016, it had a population of 3.5 million, with a literacy rate of 98% (World Bank) and annual GDP growth rate of 2.0%. According to Ramadani and Schneider (2013) from the year 2001 to 2010 in Bosnia and Herzegovina, there has been substantial economic growth, and it is due to the growth of small and medium-sized enterprises (SMEs), where out of 14,321 companies registered, only 55 or 0.38% were large enterprises.

Politically, B&H is highly decentralized state with weak state institutions (Petričević and Danis 2007), and it currently has the status of potential candidate country for joining the European Union (EU).

B&H's history of entrepreneurship is written down in famous travel writings of Čelebi (1967) that are describing his visits to Sarajevo in the year of 1660. B&H's capital Sarajevo is described as a city that became famous for its trading and merchandising activities, and it was major trading center at times. Therefore, this is one of the first insights on entrepreneurial activities in this region, and old crafts (Exhibits 3 and 4) are one of the proofs of entrepreneurial activities that have been still nurtured and preserved. These entrepreneurial activities are usually preserved within craftsman's families and have been passed on from generation to generation.

Among transition economies, Bosnia and Herzegovina presents a somewhat unique case that has the potential to provide an excellent opportunity as well as perplexing challenges, to those who aspire to do business in this turbulent economy (Petričević and Danis 2007).

Exhibit 3 Kazandžiluk street in Sarajevo, Craft shops of braziers; photo © 2017 Azra Bičo

Exhibit 4 Kovači street, Sarajevo, Craft shop of tinsmith and locksmith; photo © 2017 Azra Bičo

2 Historical Overview

The Bosnian state was first mentioned in Byzantine sources in the tenth century. In the fourteenth century, Bosnia and Herzegovina was autonomous and in the year 1377 was proclaimed a Kingdom.

Exhibit 5 Bistrik railway station building, Sarajevo; photo © 2017 Azra Bičo

Following centuries were a period of occupations. From 1463 until 1878 was a period of Ottoman occupation whose influence is still highly present in modern B&H's society. Its influence was highly felt through various aspects of life; it was the interplay of the cultures, cuisine, and many others. Majority of the population converted to Islam, so the religious influence of Ottomans was also present. Still, in modern history, these two nations are considered brotherly. In the year 1878 by the decision of Congress of Berlin, the mandate to occupy Bosnia and Herzegovina was given to Austro-Hungarian Empire, and it lasted for 40 years. During the Austro-Hungarian period of occupation, infrastructure was established, and Bosnia and Herzegovina got a railway and road network. Exhibit 5 features Bistrik railway station building's southeast facade, that was built in 1906, and is a National monument. This period was also characterized by extensive factory and mines openings. Austro Hungarians invested a lot in the schooling; many elementary and few high schools were built.

The year 1914 marked world's history as the beginning of World War I, by the assassination of Archduke Franc Ferdinand in the year 1914 at Latin Bridge in Sarajevo (Exhibit 6). In the year 1918 B&H was incorporated into the newly created Kingdom of Serbs, Croats, and Slovenes.

Anti-Fascist Council for the National Liberation of Yugoslavia known under abbreviation AVNOJ, established in November 26, 1942, had three sessions, which in 29 November 1945 resulted in formation Socialist Federal Republic of Yugoslavia (SFRY). In that same year of 1945, Bosnia and Herzegovina became part of Socialist Federal Republic of Yugoslavia (SFRY). During the World War II, Bosnia and Herzegovina was within the independent State of Croatia (NDH).

Exhibit 6 Latin Bridge; photo © 2017 Azra Bičo

Modern Bosnian and Herzegovinian history is dating from its independence that triggered a war and ended by signing and Dayton Peace Agreement that formed country into its current existence.

Bosnia and Herzegovina under Ottoman Empire was no exception to rest of the Empire when it comes to the way economy and entrepreneurship were organized. Infrastructure was quite poorly built during the times, the land was abundant, but capital and labor were scarce. B&H under Ottoman Empire was the agrarian economy. Serb population preserved their traditional Byzantine and Slavic traditions, and the Muslim population adopted Turkish-Islamic culture along with the values of the Bazaar economy. Majority of people were living and supporting themselves from their small house holdings from which tax was gathered. In the FY system, B&H was a command economy. It was a part of a larger picture to which B&H presented one of leading suppliers of minerals and metals, with almost half of its productive labor force working in heavy industry. The majority of production was oriented and planned based on the need of FY market. This period was characterized by economic prosperity and economic growth and peace. Sarajevo economically blossomed in the year 1984 when it hosted Winter Olympic. It was a first Olympic game to be held at socialist state. Although in 1980 Yugoslavia was hit by the significant crisis, this project was well developed and organized. Numerous hotels (Exhibit 7) and sports facilities (Exhibit 8) were built especially for this purpose that boosted Sarajevo's entrepreneurial scene as well.

The war that lasted for 4 years was devastating for B&H's economy; houses, schools, hospitals, mosques, and factories were demolished. To start a new life and to rebuild it, financial support was needed. Hence in this period, B&H was relying heavily on foreign aid. The war scars are still present in many cities in B&H.

Exhibit 7 Former hotel
Holiday Inn; photo © 2017
Azra Bičo

Ideas of employment that belong to previous systems where workers used to work in the single workplace in the status of an employee upon their retirement were no longer possible since the majority of production lines were shut down, and because new system does not support such ideas.

Ivy (1996) explained that most of the attention in postcommunist and transition economies are centered on the privatization of existing state-owned enterprises. Bosnia and Herzegovina is no exception to the case. Companies needed to go through the process of privatization for the public to private ownership as it is usually the case for the most transitional postwar economy. The process of privatization in Bosnia and Herzegovina is in its final phase. By the completion of this process, a new phase of private ownership is to be present at B&H's market. Ramadani et al. (2013) state the

Exhibit 8 Zetra Olympic hall; photo © 2017 Azra Bičo

more procedures there are, the more opportunities for corruption there are. This is
exactly the case of B&H. In Bosnia and Herzegovina, however, most of the formerly
state-owned industry has been damaged during the interethnic fighting. Dana (1999)
states "A free-enterprise system is not so much the result of the transfer of ownership
of existing firms. Instead, entrepreneurs are rebuilding the economy by identifying
niches and the flexible structure of new ventures." Dana (1999) also emphasizes on
the advantages of the low wage structure in Bosnia and Herzegovina, and that it could
be a competitive advantage in light manufacturing.

Ramadani and Dana (2013) identified approaches in transitioning economies.
One approach is when reform takes place gradually, to avoid side effects. The second
approach according to them is the big bang approach that prescribes closure of
money-losing state-owned industries and proclaims immediate transition to capitalism. According to Bosma and Levie (2010), Bosnia and Herzegovina belongs to a
group of efficiency-driven economies. Such economies are characterized by a
tendency to be more linked to global markets, and to achieve growth and prosperity
entrepreneurs who are growth and technology-oriented are needed in order to create
more employment opportunities.

Palalic et al. (2017) explained that even though B&H in former Yugoslavia
(FY) was one of the best former republics, and it was an industry-based republic,
its economy is in transition and passes through a very difficult time. Major problems
include infrastructure and capital assets, a lack of saving and investment, lost markets,
unstable government and financial structure, and the absence of potential employers.
There are far too few jobs for those who want one. Bosnia and Herzegovina's
unemployment is severe since it is long term and structural. It has been reported in
country's Labor Force Survey that half of all employees are unemployed for 5 years,

of which one quarter is unemployed for more than 10 years and can hardly be considered as economically active (Bičo 2016).

As noted by Julien (1993), the recovery of an economy can be linked to the growth of entrepreneurship. Ramadani et al. (2014) identified that what are the different approaches and efforts to define entrepreneurship, but they all pose these essential elements, innovation, risk-taking, a combination of production factory, creation of new enterprise, realization of profit, and ensuring a business growth.

Two terms entrepreneurship and being self-employed are mutually inclusive and of high importance for transitioning economies such as Bosnia and Herzegovina to recover and boost economy's growth.

Cantillon (1756) defined the entrepreneur the one who takes the risk of being self-employed and Fayolle (2007) identifies entrepreneurship as an engine of national Economy. Hence, the importance of the level of self-employment to be high in recovering economies is inevitable.

When it comes to entrepreneurship, small and medium businesses play an essential role. According to Labour Force survey, employment figures in the year 2016 in B&H according to Labor Force Survey showed out of a total number of people employed 75.6% were employees, 21.1% were self-employed, and unpaid family workers 2.3%. Self-employment figures preform so low due to problems of inertia and mind setting of people that are related to a safety and job security of work, due to habits to which people are accustomed to from previous economic system. This is related to comfortability and intensity of work and responsibility regarding individual results of work in the public sector, which cannot be easily compared to the ones in private sector. Insufficient level of competition in private sector that is felt especially in the period of post-economic crisis is one of the problems as well as the problem of monopolization of employment in public sector that is related to the privilege of employment opportunities that the leading political parties have.

Demirgüc-Kunt et al. (2009) identified financial constraints as the main obstacle for individuals to switch from being employed to self-employed, finding where that wealthier households with access to bank financing are more likely to become entrepreneurs and survive an early period in business and determinants for its performance.

Facing massive unemployment in the country, the promotion of self-employment and microenterprise should become country's major priority as a possibility for unemployment rates to decrease, since the self-employed can be considered as the smallest, but initially the most vital unit of entrepreneurial activity (Demirgüc-Kunt et al. 2009).

Small and medium enterprises are hoping for the development of the region, and they are the ones that boost economic growth on a smaller microscale. One of the positive examples in B&H is the town of Visoko, once famous for factory and production line KTK Visoko (factory of leather textile) (Exhibit 9), that went bankrupt. Now the town has many privately owned small craft shops designing and sewing various leather products as it can be seen in Exhibit 10. This area is also famous for meat processing industries that are most successful in Bosnia and

Exhibit 9 KTK Visoko; photo © 2017 Azra Bičo

Herzegovina, all of which privately owned. Exhibit 11 features factory and ware-house of meat processing industry Semić.

Dana and Fayolle have identified the importance of SME for countries that strive to achieve economic development since they are characterized by flexible, adaptable, relatively inexpensive to establish and close, adjustable to specific market demands, and these should be generators of economic development.

Although several towns in B&H have been a fruitful place for SME establish-ment, most of the business activities take place in Canton Sarajevo since this region is dominant in the indirect taxes collection. It is primarily because this is the central region of the country when it comes to public administration allocation.

Micro-areas in Bosnia and Herzegovina such as "Gračanica (Exhibit 12), Gradačac, and Tešanj" towns have been recognized as very fruitful areas for entre-preneurship, more specifically family businesses. These towns have low unemploy-ment rates, due to a large number of registered small and medium enterprises. (Exhibit 12 shows Euro-Galant company, leather producing goods company, that is just one of the examples of successful SME in this region.)

Džafić (2010) identified that SME in the process found it important from which it is expected to be critical pillar of economic development of Bosnia and Herzegovina. Moreover, SMEs in countries of transition such as Macedonia and B&H are facing problems of access to external sources of financing (Balling et al. 2009; Burk and

Exhibit 10 Craft shop of leather products; photo © 2017 Azra Bičo

Exhibit 11 Semić meat industry, Factory; photo © 2017 Azra Bičo

Exhibit 12 Euro-Galant Gračanica; photo © 2017 Azra Bičo

Lehmann 2006; IFC 2010). In Bosnia and Herzegovina, companies usually use bank loans as their source of financing (Petković 2010).

Business creation was not boosted and supported by governments, due to inadequate procedures. These resulted in two negativities, sizeable informal economy and lowered foreign direct investment figures. To attract foreign and domestic investors, firstly it is necessary to create a favorable business environment, which is the case for Bosnia and Herzegovina and Macedonia (Hisrich et al. 2016) During postwar period, major Foreign Direct Investment came into banking sector, and in these years, Bosnia and Herzegovina experienced GDP growth (Bastic 2004); in 1990, B&H started its transition process via economic liberalization and the development and implementation of market-oriented reforms aimed at achieving long-term growth.

One of the ways to overcome current problems is the process of reindustrialization that should stop the process of depopulation and prevent depopulation of the B&H that has been of country's major concern over past 10 years, along with a current unfavorable trend of brain drain.

3 Environment for Entrepreneurship

After a destructive war from 1992 to 1995, no infrastructure was left, from which the state can start its development. However, a little freedom after the war animated the beginning of entrepreneurship in Bosnia and Herzegovina. Bosnians, mainly males, were looking to contribute to their families' welfare, and these goals started to create an entrepreneurial environment in Bosnia. Through the time, more and more people were engaged in entrepreneurial transactions, and Bosnian economy is being developed by small entrepreneurs (Dana 1999). This hard time created strong entrepreneurs with a strong mindset whose businesses are now very well developed and employ hundreds of people. In the first decade after the war, taking into consideration of existing constraints, entrepreneurship was gradually developing. In late 2000s, many jobs were created. People, capital, and goods were moving more easily and, for instance, shifting from one job to another was relatively easy if the war consequences were taken into account.

The global crisis in 2008 affected Bosnian entrepreneurship development in which many firms were straggled to cover up firms' daily operations. Lots of them were looking for a mode how to overcome these transactions problems. These issues were very serious, and they went to the extent that the existence of their families will be affected if they do not find a way to respond to firm's payables. It is because their business was mainly financed by themselves from their savings (Dana and Ramadani 2015; Palalic 2017).

Transition process in Bosnia and Herzegovina started in 1990 but prolonged until now. One of the steps that were done in the early stage is establishing an authority that will be in charge of it. In Federation BiH, it is "Agencija za privatizaciju u Federaciji BiH—FPA" (Agency for privatization for Federation of BiH). In Republika Srpska, in charge of it is "Investiciono razvojna banka Republike Srpske IRBRS" (Investment Development Bank of RS). The FPA was established in 1997 while IRBRS in 2006. Both agencies are under the authority of respective entity of Bosnia and Herzegovina. Federation BiH also has cantonal privatization agencies which manage privatization at the cantonal level.

Entrepreneurship in Bosnia still needs more freedom from the State. Doing business in Bosnia is still in the shadow and does not appear very easy compared to ex-Yugoslavia republics. Doing business, which depicts how easy or complicated it is to do business for entrepreneurs in a country, shows that Bosnia is the last one among ex-Yugoslavian republics, 86th. Still, procedures are time-consuming for local entrepreneurs. However, compared to 2012, in 2017 "Bosnia and Herzegovina made starting a business easier by reducing the paid-in minimum capital requirement for limited liability companies and increasing the efficiency of the notary system (Doing Business 2017, p. 21)." If a business is characterized by a significant investment, where for instance, requires a warehouse, then only for getting electricity an entrepreneur needs to spend 126 days to complete that procedure with a very high cost (Doing Business 2017, pp. 44–46).

Entrepreneurship development in Bosnia lacks institutional support across the country. The challenges and obstacles have been discussed in the early Bosnian transition by Dana (1999) and Dana and Dana (2003) and recently by Džafić et al. (2011), Palalic (2017), and Palalic et al. (2017). Governmental support is inevitable to create a *business lake* which will be the critical source of social and economic development of B&H.

4   Overview of SMEs' Structure in B&H

"KDBiH"[1] stands for the classification of all economic activities in B&H related to SMEs, micro, and large enterprises, which is made on the basis of "Statistical Nomenclature economic activities of the European Union (NACE Rev.1.14)"[2] and is comparable with the international standard Industrial Classification of all economic activities of the United Nations (ISIC Rev.3).[3] NACE is a full statistical classification of economic activities of the European Union, NACE Rev. 1.1, which is only elaborated further to the level of the subclass (code defined by the five digits). These subclasses reflect the specifics of B&H, in particular with its two entities (the Federation of B&H and Republika Srpska) and a separate administrative unit of the Brčko District of B&H. So all private entities, enterprises, firms, and organizations have been given a code of activity, namely, "KD." The "KDB&H" or NACE (in EU) category has the following hierarchical grouping of economic and other activities:

1. Section (indicated by single alphabetic code)
2. Subsection (indicated by two-letter alphabetic code)
3. Division (marked by two-digit numerical code)
4. Group (designated three-digit numerical code)
5. Class (indicated by four-digit numerical code)
6. Subclass (indicated by five-digit numerical code).

So, the Classification of Economic Activities (KDB&H), or NACE, consists of 17 sections, 31 sub-sections, the division of 62,224 groups, 514 classes, and 625 sub-classes (Table 1).

According to a report (First Release 2017, p. 2) from Agency for Statistics of B&H, "a classification of enterprises by employment size classes, using criteria "number of persons employed," shows that microenterprises (0–9 persons employed) create the most significant share of the total number of classified enterprises, even 74.1%. Small enterprises (10–49 persons employed) create 18.4%, medium enterprises (50–249 persons employed) create 6.3%, while the share of large enterprises (250 and more persons employed) is only 1.0%. For 0.2% of active enterprises, data on employment are not available."

Regarding the definition of SME in B&H, it is very similar to the EU definition of SME, which is according to some employees, turnover or balance sheet total. In Table 2, the definitions of SMEs in B&H are provided.

Microenterprises are those who employ less than ten employees with a turnover of less than 2 million euros (with the same balance sheet total). *Small* enterprises are defined between 10 and 49 with the turnover less than 10 million euros (with the same balance sheet total). *Medium-sized* companies are those who employ between

---

[1]KDBiH is "klasifikacija djelatnosti u BiH".

[2]Available at http://ec.europa.eu

[3]Available at http://unstats.un.org

Table 1 The basic structure and number of titles of "KDB&H" or NACE, by hierarchical levels

Names of the sections of "KDB&H"	Number of titles of "KDB&H" or "NACE", by hierarchical levels				Sub-class		
	Sub sections	Divisions	Groups	Class	Total	Elaborated	Non-elaborated
Agriculture, hunting, and forestry	1	2	6	14	25	18	7
Fishing	1	1	1	2	3	2	1
Mining and quarrying	2	5	13	16	21	9	12
Manufacturing	14	23	103	242	254	24	230
Production and supply of electricity	1	2	4	7	10	4	6
Electricity, gas, and water supply							
Construction	1	1	5	17	21	7	14
Wholesales and retails; repair of motor vehicles, motorcycles, and items for personal and household goods	1	3	19	79	98	28	70
Catering	1	1	5	8	15	11	4
Transport, storage, and communication	1	5	14	21	24	6	18
Financial intermediation	1	3	5	12	14	4	10
Real estate, renting, and business	1	5	23	39	43	8	35
Public administration and defense; necessary social security	1	1	3	10	37	34	3
Education	1	1	4	6	10	6	4
Health and social work	1	1	3	7	14	11	3
Other community, social and personal	1	4	12	30	32	4	28
Service activities							
Households' activities	1	3	3	3	3	0	3
Territorial organizations and bodies	1	1	1	1	1	0	1
TOTAL (17 sections)	31	62	224	514	625	176	449

Table 2 Definition of SMEs in B&H

Company category	Employees	Turnover (€)	Balance sheet total (€)
Micro	<10	<2 million	<2 million
Small	<50	<10 million	<10 million
Medium-sized	<250	<50 million	<43million

Source: EU Commission (2013)

50 and 249 employees with a turnover of less than 50 million euros (with balance sheet total of <43 million euros).

According to the state Agency for Statistics, an SME's definition is based on the following criteria: *"Data on the number of persons employed are classified in classes by size, according to the relevant EU regulations in: micro (0–9 persons), small (10–49 persons), medium (50–249 persons) and large (250 and more persons employed); and "data on the amount of revenue are classified in classes by size in micro (0–3,999,999 km), small (4,000,000–19,999,999 km), medium (20,000,000–99,999,999 km) and large (100,000,000 and more km)"*.

Types of companies in BiH are regulated by The Company Law of the Federation of B&H (Official Gazette of FBiH No. 81/15), and the Company Law of Republic of Srpska (Official Gazette of RS No. 127/08, 58/09,100/11 and 67/13) regulates the establishment, operation, and termination of businesses in BiH (Table 3).

5 B&H's Economy at Glance

The macroeconomic picture of B&H is not so good. The two entities and one district make the aggregate gross domestic product (GDP) which in 2015 was 28.522 million km, while GDP per Capita was 8107 km. Export in 2016 was 9418.109 km, and import amounted to 16,161.014 km. The aggregate deficit of B&H's economy was 6742.905 km.

The following table (Table 4) depicts how much each entity of B&H and one district contribute to the aggregate GDP of the country. Federation of BiH has throughout 10 years contributed a double amount compared to RS. While Brcko District has the negligible amount compared to the two entities.

Salaries in Bosnia and Herzegovina (Table 5) are quite low, which shows a right place for foreign investors. Salaries in B&H compared to EU are much lower. However, salary range in other ex-Yugoslavia republics is more or less the same (except Slovenia and Croatia). The following table shows the gradual increase in salaries in B&H from 2000 to August 2017. Apparently, an increase in salaries within these 16.8 years was observed, like almost triple. Nonetheless, this amount is not even near to the EU's one, to which B&H streams for the last decade.

When it comes to the FDI Stock by countries, the most substantial share still refers to Austria (1275 million km), Croatia (1140 million km), and Serbia (1082 million km). With Slovenia, it is 486 million km, Russia 417 million km,

Table 3 Types of companies in BiH

Type company	Federation of BiH	RS of BiH
Unlimited joint liability company (d.n.o./o.d)	Founded by the establishment contract of two or more partners, domestic or foreign, natural persons only. Founders are liable to use all their assets, including personal property. There are no requirements for minimum or maximum contributions	Founded by the establishment act of two or more domestic/foreign natural and/or legal partners who commit to do certain activity under the same company name, with their own unlimited solidary liability for company commitments. There are no requirements for minimum or maximum contributions
Limited liability company (d.o.o.)	Founded by the establishment act or establishment contact by one or more domestic/foreign natural and/or legal entities with initial capital divided into parts. A member in a limited company is liable for the value of his investment in that company. Minimum initial capital is 1000 BAM (approx. 500 euros);	Founded by the establishment act of 1–100 domestic/foreign natural and/or legal entities. Shareholder in a limited company is not personally liable for any of the debts of the company, other than for the value of his investment in that company. Minimum initial capital is 1 BAM (approx. 0.5 euros)
Limited partnership (k.d.)	Company founded by the establishment contract of two or more domestic/foreign natural and/or legal entities. There must be at least 1 partner with full liability (including private property) and at least 1 partner with limited liability, the liability being limited by the value of his share in that company. There are no requirements for minimum or maximum initial capital	Founded of two or more domestic/ foreign natural and/or legal entities by the establishment act; one person at least has unlimited liability for the company, and one person at least has liability to the amount of his/her investment in the company. There are no requirements for minimum or maximum initial capital
Joint-stock company (d.d./a.d.)	Legal entities founded by the establishment contract of one or more domestic/foreign natural or legal shareholders with initial capital divided into shares. (1) Open joint-stock company is a legal entity (banks and insurance companies or company with minimum initial capital of 4,000,000 BAM, i.e., 2,000,000 euros, and 40 shareholders at least) whose shares may be publicly listed. (2) Closed joint-stock company is a legal entity, whose shares are distributed among a limited number of shareholders. The minimum initial capital is 50,000 BAM (25,000 euros).	Legal entity founded by the establishment act of one or more domestic/foreign natural and/or legal entities with initial capital divided into a defined number of shares. (1) Open joint-stock company is a legal entity, whose shares may be publicly traded, i.e., offers its shares for sale upon the open market and they are listed on the stock exchanges and other public markets. The minimum initial capital is 50,000 BAM (25,000 euros). (2) Closed joint-stock company is a legal entity, whose shares are distributed among a limited number of shareholders. The minimum initial capital is 20,000 BAM (10,000 euros).

Source: FIPA BiH (2017)

Table 4 Share of entities in GDP of B&H, 2006–2015

BDP entity/year	2006	2007	2008	2009	2010	2011	2012	2013	2014	% 2015
BDP za BiH/GDP for BiH	100.00	100.00	100.00	100.00	100.00	100.00	100.00	100.00	100.00	100.00
BDP za Federaciju BiH/GDP for FBiH	65.02	64.94	64.41	64.52	64.94	64.58	64.95	64.97	65.24	65.48
BDP za Republiku Srpsku/GDP for RS	32.63	32.61	33.29	33.24	32.82	33.13	32.78	32.76	32.40	32.09
BDP za Brčko Distrikt/GDP for Brcko district	2.35	2.45	2.30	2.24	2.24	2.29	2.27	2.27	2.36	2.43

Source: Agency for Statistics of B&H (2017), (Thematic Bulletin 01, p. 22)

Table 5 Average salaries in B&H from 2000 to 2017

Average net salary in BiH by months and years

	I	II	III	IV	V	VI	VII	VIII	IX	X	XI	XII	KM average
2000	335	349	363	369	365	364	373	379	388	385	398	384	372
2001	401	401	398	398	403	403	403	410	415	422	421	425	409
2002	433	434	437	440	444	441	449	447	454	457	456	463	446
2003	476	475	473	479	481	484	486	487	488	488	499	486	484
2004	496	495	494	499	506	509	506	509	506	508	511	521	505
2005[a]	522	529	530	526	533	536	538	543	543	546	549	561	538
2006	570	560	571	577	581	584	586	591	592	599	601	613	586
2007	614	617	625	635	643	641	642	651	652	661	672	681	645
2008	677	716	726	739	753	748	763	764	775	780	776	798	752
2009	784	790	790	794	786	793	792	785	785	789	791	802	790
2010	789	782	798	799	795	798	799	800	800	795	805	818	798
2011	807	799	818	811	821	820	813	822	814	813	824	828	816
2012	826	818	823	823	836	822	827	830	813	831	832	831	826
2013	829	815	819	824	832	822	830	828	826	833	828	838	827
2014	838	822	826	832	830	829	836	825	826	834	823	843	830
2015	828	820	832	833	830	834	838	826	828	826	826	842	830
2016	829	829	843	830	838	837	832	843	837	837	847	853	838
2017	846	838	854	839	860	851	849	858					

[a]Since 2005 Brčko District BiH included
Source: Agency for Statistic B&H (2017)

Netherlands 371 million km, Germany 286 million km, Italy 284 million km, Switzerland 258 million km, UK 229 million km, and others 801 million km (Exhibit 13).

Foreign investments in Bosnia and Herzegovina fluctuated from year to year. The highest FDI flow happened in 2014, and the lowest was in 2013. 2016 was lower than 2015. When we observe the 1st quarter of each year from 2012 to 2017, it shows that 2013 was the highest flow. In 2017, this tendency shows fair level compared to 2012, 2015, and 2016 (Exhibit 14).

6   Toward the Future

Geo-strategic position of Bosnia and Herzegovina makes the country able to perform better than reports showed in recent years. Wealthy with natural sources, Bosnia could make decent progress regarding its economic development. The country still suffers from a deficit in its national accounts, which makes investments and spending within itself difficult. As reports show, overall, it is making a gradual progress, but it is not enough to keep pace with other republics in Ex-Yugoslavia region.

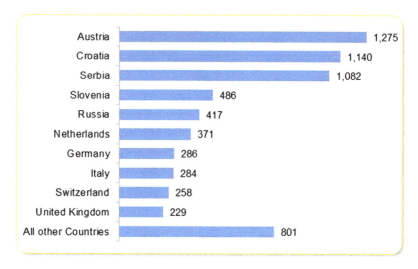

Exhibit 13 Top investor countries in B&H, May 1994–December 2016 (in km million). Source: FIPA (2017)

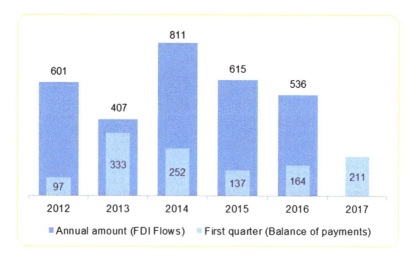

Exhibit 14 Foreign Direct Investment (FDI) flows in B&H, per first quarter and annually, 2012–2017. Source: FIPA (2017)

Entrepreneurship development in Bosnia and Herzegovina is in an initial phase. Entrepreneurs still face difficulties in many segments of starting a new business. Taxes posed by the Government are still huge (Palalic 2017). Liquidity of SMEs is very low. Some of the receivables are looked forward to being paid for even up to 200 days. The life cycle is made to be very distracted, and insolvency of SMEs is common. Not to wait for a long time to get receivables, many firms take a strategic tactic to improvise it with compensation of other goods or services available with the business partner (supplier, client, and similar). This *improvization* makes challenging to develop and grow SME sector. Problems occur when they go internationally; they are not able to get settled transactions between them and international partners. On the other side, the State is not strong enough to give such support. Additionally, due to high taxes, many potential entrepreneurs reject to be self-employed and to employ other people. Moreover, the State still has no sensibility toward this issue.

Despite these limbo business circumstances, Bosnia and Herzegovina has progressed a lot regarding tourism. Compared to the late 1990s, the number of tourists is almost increased by four times. Every year this number increases and Bosnia and Herzegovina seemed to be an attractive place for the rest of the world. Along with this, many micro and small start-ups are established which offer services to tourists across the country. Rural and women entrepreneurship is increasing every year. The manufacturing business is also doing a good progress, and it is mainly exported to the EU countries, and according to Agency for Statistic of B&H, it contributes 34% of the total GDP of B&H. Moreover, this shows that the *real sector* (production) is at the highest level for now, but not in full capacities compared to the time of ex-Yugoslavia.

Challenges for entrepreneurship exist. However, prospective entrepreneurs should believe in future success because Bosnia and Herzegovina has all circumstances (row materials and others) to keep it small and slowly develop through the time.

Bosnia and Herzegovina faces another serious challenge which is population. Young people, single and married, are trying to reside in other countries, to live it up for the rest of their life. It is a red alarm for the state to keep this rate low and to increase a population number. The market of 3.8 million is not big so that one can *observe and do nothing*. The youth of Bosnia and Herzegovina is its legacy, and politics in Bosnia should seriously acknowledge this.

7   Case Study: MIBRAL LLC[4]

Ms. MBS[5] is a director of MIBRAL LLC (limited liability company) in Bosnia and Herzegovina. She has completed bachelor studies in Austria, and MA in Australia, with specialization in Human Resources (HR), where she was working in mining, and in construction (Exhibits 15 and 16) industries, with 10 years of relevant work experience. From the year 2011 onwards, she is director of firm MIBRAL LLC. The company has 40 years long history, and it is a *family company* started by Ms. MBS's father, Mr. MB.[6] The company changed many forms of corporate structures, wherein

---

[4]This case is written by Azra Bičo based on conversation with the company's CEO.

[5]MBS are initials of a lady who wished to display only her initials and who leads the company now. For more information, you can visit http://mibral.ba/

[6]MB are initials of MBS's father. He also wished to display his initials only.

Exhibit 15 Mibral LLC team at construction site; photo © MIBRAL LLC

Exhibit 16 MIBRAL LLC at construction site; photo © MIBRAL LLC

socialism was first registered as a crafts shop, then as a private company, followed by sole proprietorship, and finally, in the year of 2001, they changed their form of organization to the existing one—*MIBRAL LLC*. It is exclusively project-oriented firm, where the number of employees depends exclusively on some obtained projects.

Much time is devoted to internal organization starting as from administration, technical preparation for projects, finance, information technologies. Work of the company is combined with office and field work, performed by a team of around of 20 employees, who collaborate jointly in drafting, preparing, and implementing these projects that are complementing each other. In field work, MIBRAL LLC employs *construction technicians*, *leading masters*, *drivers*, and *assisting workers*. All these workers are very important, and if they present themselves through their performance as efficient and hardworking that is very crucial for the company, and they are to be kept in company's team, even during the winter season, when they do not perform a lot of work. In that part of operations, the company has 40–60 workers among of which some are loyal and been working with the company for 20 years so far. Human capital is highly important and valued in this company, and by all means, they try to keep them as part of their team, by investing in their education/training skills.

Most of the business activities done in MIBRAL LLC, precisely 95% of them, are construction work. Most important projects done by MIBRAL LLC are dating back to mid-1980s, at those times it was private company MB that had carried out works on three bridges on the Krivaja River Zavidovići, which were vital projects in that period. After the war in Bosnia and Herzegovina, the focus was on the balance and development, the arrival of foreign investors, and the expansion of the financial options of these domestic companies enabled MIBRAL LLC to participate in a variety of public projects. The company worked on the infrastructure in the heart of the city of Sarajevo, and that is company's contribution to all citizens, as well as for tourists, namely the streets in the old town of Baščaršija, Bravadžiluk, Sarači, and part of the Ferhadija street that MIBRAL LLC did. MIBRAL LLC is the leader in the Canton of Sarajevo in the area of construction works, but the problem with the nature of the work is that they are invisible (underground works), yet very important for everything. Now, with current water restrictions, we all understand this problem probably better. On the other hand, company's other works such as regulation of river flows, sanitation of landslips, and construction works of high-rise buildings are evident. Company's core business is low construction, water supply, sewerage, reconstruction of landslips, and regulation of water flows.

The company has a 1-year strategic plan, and currently, they are working on a 3-year strategic plan. The operational plan is designed at an annual level. The prices that company offers are very low since the projects would fail if they were not efficient regarding the organization, planning, and budgeting.

When it comes to plans of company's long-term strategy, like mergers and acquisition, Ms. MBS said that in the short run it is certainly not in their plan. However, for the market, as it is, the bigger projects are more and more present. So the firm, by its capacities, shows that the operational and technical standards must meet the criteria for the tenders. They believe that there are in the company, enough skilled people to get those capacities, by how much the company can finance itself. *Mergers* are not excluded, but it is not in their 3-year strategy. However, in the long term, as far as the projects are concerned, this is very current and ongoing thing, and they have already worked on several projects jointly with partners, and without the right key partners, they cannot achieve satisfactory technical and financial conditions.

Also to respond to market demands, company very often goes into the form of a joint venture tender, with certain partner companies. On such projects, jobs are complementary; every project as a project has parts that company cannot satisfy/fulfill so that coworkers/partnering companies step in. The company is depending on 90% public procurement, because it is dealing with infrastructure projects. Therefore, all works are reduced to public works, given the infrastructure issues; all projects are mostly financed by the European Development Bank, European Investment Bank, World Bank, but all procedures go through the institutes and municipalities.

Company possesses ISO standard certificates, since in MIBRAL LLC they respect each contract regarding the time achievement of works, timeframes, and have a flexible attitude regarding the requirements of the investor. Regardless that they lack support from relevant state bodies, MIBRAL LLC relies on productivity and flexibility of their operative and they are sure that they will succeed in doing business positively.

In a context of innovations, technologies of work, materialization, it cannot be expected to be achieved without the involvement of others. Thanks to continuous investments, the absence of a decisive plan, wheres in the last 2 years company has doubled their fixed assets, more modern machinery was bought. When selecting materials and tender regulations, there is a certain number of certificates, specifications, some guarantees that company always requires ensuring quality. It is because in the end company is the one that gives a guarantee, which means that each project is an investment, each project is different, no matter how many of them looks the same and requires different methodologies of work. One of the company's aims is to direct the capacities from internal existing structures, training of deficit craftsmen to keep company running, as well as to be able to expand company's activity and to expand overall in the business.

Company's success is measured in various ways besides profit. Beneficial are ISO standards that company has introduced and implemented; it is essential to certify and recertify, it is essential that company operate at the level of them in that compliance. By them, it means, specifically, the Balance Score Card is the right way to measure company's success. These parameters come from company's processes, type of machines, the success of bids, public procurements in the field of public procurements in percentages are monitored, how many offers how many jobs, finished jobs without any complaints, and everything is concerning the parameters.

Marketing to a company is essential (at least for a small segment of housing construction). However, overly, the conclusive answer is no, due to a nature of the job. Some of the tenders of bidding on public calls have a prevailing decision on the amount of business activities company will perform, which citizens do not know about, the company has 10–15 key buyers/investors with whom they are cooperating, so in these circles, marketing is not necessary.

The key goal of MIBRAL LLC is to maintain leading position at Sarajevo Canton, and special accent is given to the water supply, and sewage system works, to maintain a leading position in this area of business activity.

References

Balling, M., Bernet, B., & Gnan, E. (2009). *"Financing SMEs in Europe", SUERF – The European money and finance forum Vienna.* Retrieved February 18, 2014, from http://imap.suerf.org/download/studies/study20093.pdf

Bastic, M. (2004). Success factors in transition countries. *European Journal of Innovation Management, 7*(1), 65–79.

Bičo, A. (2016). Economic aspects of unemployment in Bosnia and Herzegovina. In Y. Oğurlu & A. Kulanić (Eds.), *Bosnia and Herzegovina: Law, society and politics* (pp. 167–178). Ilidža: Sabah Print.

Bičo, A., & Bajram, N. (2012). *Economic policies for business: Case of Bosnia and Herzegovina.* In 5th International Scientific-Technical Conference Business Development 2012: Economic policy & business of small and medium enterprises, Zenica, BIH; 11/2012.

Bosma, N. S., & Levie, J. (2010). *Global entrepreneurship monitor 2009 executive report.*

Burk, J. E., & Lehmann, R. P. (2006). *Financing your small business.* Naperville: Sphinx Publishing.

Cantillon, R. (1756). *Essaisur la nature du commerce en général.* London: Chez Fletcher Gyles.

Čelebi, E. (1967). *Putopis. Odlomci o jugoslovenskim zemljama.* Preveo, uvodi komentar napisao H. Sabanović. Sarajevo.

Dana, L. P. (1999). Business and entrepreneurship in Bosnia-Herzegovina. *Journal of Business and Entrepreneurship, 11*(2), 105–109.

Dana, L. P., & Dana, T. (2003). Management and enterprise development in post-communist economies. *International Journal of Management and Enterprise Development, 1*(1), 45–54.

Dana, L. P., & Ramadani, V. (Eds.). (2015). *Family business in transition economies.* Cham: Springer.

Demirgüc-Kunt, A., Klapper, L. F., & Panos, G. A. (2009). *Entrepreneurship in post-conflict transition.* The role of informality and access to finance, World Bank policy research working paper, 4935.

Džafić, Z. (2010). *Mala i srednja preduzeća u funkciji restrukturiranja tranzicionih privreda, sa posebnim osvrtom na BiH.*

Džafić, Z., Zahirović, S., Okiĉić, J., & Kožarić, A. (2011). Internal and external obstacles to the development of SMEs in Bosnia and Herzegovina. *Croatian Economic Survey, 13*(1), 143–171.

Fayolle, A. (2007). *Entrepreneurship and new value creation: The dynamic of the entrepreneurial process.* In EBHA conference, Barcelona, Spain, Cambridge University Press, September 16–18, 2004.

Hisrich, R. D., Petković, S., Ramadani, V., & Dana, L. P. (2016). Venture capital funds in transition countries: Insights from Bosnia and Herzegovina and Macedonia. *Journal of Small Business and Enterprise Development, 23*(2), 296–315.

Ilgün, E., & Coşkun, A. (2009). *Foreign direct investments in Bosnia and Herzegovina: Banking sector example.*

Ivy, R. L. (1996). Global perspectives: Small scale entrepreneurs and private sector development in the Slovak Republic. *Journal of Small Business Management, 34*(4), 77.

Julien, P. A. (1993). Small businesses as a research subject: Some reflections on knowledge of small businesses and its effects on economic theory. *Small Business Economics, 5*(2), 157–166.

Palalic, R. (2017). The phenomenon of entrepreneurial leadership in gazelles and mice: A qualitative study from Bosnia and Herzegovina. *World Review of Entrepreneurship, Management and Sustainable Development, 13*(2/3), 211–236.

Palalic, R., Ramadani, V., & Dana, L. P. (2017). Entrepreneurship in Bosnia and Herzegovina: Focus on gender. *European Business Review, 29*(4), 476–496.

Petković, S. (2010). *Small and medium-sized enterprises in the function of economic performance (projected on the republic of Srpska)*. Unpublished doctoral dissertation, Banja Luka: Faculty of Economics, University of Banja Luka.

Petričević, O., & Danis, W. M. (2007). Bosnia and Herzegovina: Navigating a turbulent business environment. *Thunderbird International Business Review, 49*(4), 417–443.

Ramadani, V., & Dana, L. P. (2013). The state of entrepreneurship in the Balkans: Evidence from selected countries. In *Entrepreneurship in the Balkans* (pp. 217–250). Berlin: Springer.

Ramadani, V., & Schneider, R. (2013). *Entrepreneurship in the Balkans*. Cham: Springer.

Ramadani, V., Gërguri, S., Dana, L. P., & Tašaminova, T. (2013). Women entrepreneurs in the republic of Macedonia: Waiting for directions. *International Journal of Entrepreneurship and Small Business, 19*(1), 95–121.

Ramadani, V., Rexhepi, G., Gërguri-Rashiti, S., Ibraimi, S., & Dana, L. P. (2014). Ethnic entrepreneurship in Macedonia: The case of Albanian entrepreneurs. *International Journal of Entrepreneurship and Small Business, 23*(3), 313–335.

Websites

Agency for Statistics of Bosnia and Herzegovina. (2017). Retrieved November 20, 2017, from http://www.bhas.ba/index.php?option=com_publikacija&view=publikacija_pregled&ids=2&id=11&n=Nati&Itemid=&lang=en

EU Comission. (2013). Accessed November 10, 2017, from https://ec.europa.eu/commission/index_en

Fisrt release, B&H gency for statistics. (2017). Accessed November 20, 2017, from http://www.bhas.ba/saopstenja/2017/DEM_01_2017_Q2_0_BS.pdf

FIPA BiH. (2017). Accessed November 15, 2017, from http://www.fipa.gov.ba/default.aspx?langTag=bs-BA&template_id=123&pageIndex=1

FIPA. (2017). Accessed November 15, 2017, from http://www.fipa.gov.ba/default.aspx?langTag=bs-BA&template_id=123&pageIndex=1

International Finance Corporation (IFC). (2010). *Scaling-up SME access to financial services in the developing world*. Retrieved from www.gpfi.org/sites/default/files/documents/G20_Stocktaking_Report_0.pdf

Ramo Palalić is an Assistant Professor at the Management Program, Faculty of Business and Administration, International University of Sarajevo, Sarajevo, Bosnia and Herzegovina. His research interests are entrepreneurship, leadership, marketing, and management. He teaches at both undergraduate and postgraduate levels in the above areas. Apart from this, he is actively involved in business projects in the areas of entrepreneurial leadership and marketing management, in private and public organizations. He has authored and coauthored several articles in the reputable international journals. Currently, he is serving a few journals as reviewer/editor board member.

Azra Bičo has graduated as Bachelor of Economics at Department of Economics and Management at International University of Sarajevo in 2010, and her MA was attained in the year of 2014 at the same institution in the field of Economics as well. Azra Bičo is the author of a number of scientific papers, presented at international scientific conferences. Currently, she is working as senior assistant at Department of Economics and Management at International University of Sarajevo. She has been assisting and lecturing Macroeconomics course, Labor Economics, International Economics course and Growth and Development. Her research interests include Labor Economics, Macroeconomics and Gender studies in relation to Labor Economics.

Entrepreneurship in Croatia

Mirela Alpeza, Suncica Oberman Peterka, and Maja Has

Abstract The Republic of Croatia is situated in the southern part of Central Europe and the northern part of the Mediterranean. A good strategic position positioned Croatia throughout history as the backbone of international routes, which contributed to its economic development. Small and medium enterprises are an important segment of the Croatian economy, because of its share in the total number of enterprises (99.7% in 2015), share in total revenues (54%), employment (69.2%) and total exports (50.3%). The results of international research in which Croatia has been involved for many years (Global Entrepreneurship Monitor, Doing Business, Global Competitiveness Report, Corruption Perceptions Index) are pointing out the key challenges for further development of the small and medium enterprise sector in Croatia: insufficient level of activity in new business venture start-up, small share of growing enterprises, administrative obstacles to the implementation of entrepreneurial activity, insufficient development of the financial market and lack of education focused on the development of entrepreneurial knowledge and skills. From the perspective of achieving the targets of Europe 2020 and the perspective of the European Semester, the development of the Croatian economy, and thus the small and medium enterprise sector in the future period, will depend on the responses to the identified challenges.

1 Introduction

The Republic of Croatia is situated in the southern part of Central Europe and the northern part of the Mediterranean. It borders with Slovenia and Hungary in the north, Montenegro in the south, Serbia and Bosnia and Herzegovina in the east and with Italy in the west. The land area is 56,594 km^2, and the coastal sea area is

M. Alpeza (✉) · S. O. Peterka
Faculty of Economics in Osijek, J.J. Strossmayer University of Osijek, Osijek, Croatia
e-mail: malpeza@efos.hr; suncica@efos.hr

M. Has
Faculty of Economics and Business, University of Zagreb, Zagreb, Croatia

© Springer International Publishing AG, part of Springer Nature 2018
R. Palalić et al. (eds.), *Entrepreneurship in Former Yugoslavia*,
https://doi.org/10.1007/978-3-319-77634-7_3

31,479 km², which classifies it as a medium-sized European country (Croatian Bureau of Statistics 2016: 46). Croatia is characterised by an exceptionally rich and vivid history. From the seventh century until independence in 1991, and joining the European Union in 2013, many political structures and communities followed in succession on Croatian soil, which shaped the economy, culture and art and the social life of the population. However, Central European and Mediterranean cultural circles have had the most significant cultural impact.

There is no systematic and concise review of the historical development of entrepreneurship in Croatia, but the rich history allows highlighting relevant events and persons, which could support and enrich the knowledge about the development of Croatian entrepreneurship.

2 Historical Overview

At the beginning of the fourteenth century, Croatia was divided between Venice and Hungary. The 1300–1500 period is characterised by the development of Mediterranean trade and economy on the eastern Adriatic coast, especially in Dubrovnik, which gained independence from Venice in 1358 (Stipetic 2001: 47). The specific location of Dubrovnik allowed for the development of trade, along with which cloth making and coin mint are mentioned, as the two most significant Dubrovnik craft activities of that time. One of the most important historical figures of the fifteenth century is Dubrovnik's Benedikt Kotruljevic. His most famous work "The Book on the Art of Trade" is the first known systematic overview of the basis of market principles, social function of trade and trade practice with suggestions for its improvement. In addition to setting up the foundations of trade and entrepreneurship, emphasising the importance of recording business changes and business bookkeeping of traders of the time, Kotruljevic was the first author in world literature to seriously deal with and promote the use of double entry bookkeeping (Stipetic 2001: 153).

In the late fifteenth and throughout the sixteenth century, Croatia was in a difficult economic situation. Apart from the expansion of boundaries of the Ottoman Empire to the west, it was also faced with the shifting of the centre of world trade from the Mediterranean to the Atlantic. Trade that previously enabled the prosperity of Mediterranean cities was endangered, as well as shipbuilding and some other activities. The continental Croatia was also burdened by similar problems. In addition to war events, it was hit by the plague and great hunger. The unenviable circumstances in which Croatia lived during the sixteenth century put the primary focus on survival on the restless border, while economic development was neglected in this period.

After the Battle of Mohács (1526) and the Ottoman penetration, Croatia severed connections with the east and became increasingly open to the west and north. It is the period it became a part of the Habsburg Monarchy, which largely determined the Croatian institutional framework in the coming years. It is almost impossible to understand the development of the Croatian society during the eighteenth century outside the political, social and cultural-intellectual environments of Vienna, Buda or Bratislava as the largest urban communities of the Habsburg Monarchy (Horbec 2013: 428).

Croatian National Revival is the name of the national, cultural and political movement that marked the first half of the nineteenth century. It was the answer to the then economic, social and political events, driven by the process of forming European nations that marked the nineteenth century. The goal of the revival was the political and cultural freedom and unification of all Croats. The economic views of the mentioned revival were formulated the most profoundly by Janko Draškovic. His work "Dissertation[1]" provides a national–political programme that significantly deals with economic policy. It especially elaborates on the trade policy, relationship towards craft, agriculture, education and tax issues.

In the second half of the nineteenth century, Croatia was still divided into historical provinces, which were ruled by the powers outside Croatia. Dalmatia and Istria were under Austrian rule, and Croatia and Slavonia, together with Medjimurje and Baranja, were part of Hungary. In the economic history of Croatia, the second half of the nineteenth century marks the beginning of a new era, with faster development of the economy on capitalist foundations. The revolutionary events of 1848/1849 brought about the abolition of feudal relations to Croatia: abolition of serfdom and transformation of former feudal and serf estates into private estates (Stipetic 2013: 29). The end of the nineteenth and the beginning of the twentieth century was marked by the increase in agricultural production. For centuries, agricultural production has been focused only on local needs, but thanks to the construction of roads and better traffic connections, the situation changed significantly. Manufacturers are beginning to produce for "far-off" markets and thus enter the world market. The 1870 census shows that 42,450 people were employed in crafts, manufacturing and industry in Croatia and Slavonia (only 1% of active population) (Stipetic 2013: 31). Almost all industry was concentrated in Rijeka, Osijek, Zagreb, Karlovac and Varaždin. Craft processing of wood, stone, leather, metal and iron, fabric and fur was developed in the continental parts of the country, while large companies developed on the Croatian coast. The shipbuilding industry, which was associated with the Austro-Hungarian strategic objective of entering the Mediterranean and other seas, was particularly important. A shipyard was built in Rijeka, which built numerous steamboats, but also met the needs of the Austro-Hungarian Navy, as well as the world's first torpedo factory, which supplied navies throughout the world (Stipetic 2013: 29). In contrast to large coastal industries, many small companies in wood, textile and construction industries were important in Slavonia and Croatia at the time.

Blaz Lorkovic, the most prominent Croatian economics writer of the nineteenth century, in his most famous work "Principles of political economy or general economic science", systematically presents fundamental economic principles and

---

[1]Dissertation, or Treatise, given to the honourable lawful deputies and future legislators of our Kingdoms, delegated to the future Hungarian Diet (1832).

concepts. Lorkovic was the first in Croatia to define an entrepreneur as a person who unifies the necessary production forces (factors) and manages them in order to generate profit, knowingly assuming the danger (risk) that this production can bring. He considers the individual as the carrier of entrepreneurship because his success is a result of a well-chosen job, hard work and perseverance (Skrtic 2006: 4).

The First World War left great consequences on the Croatian economy and caused economic stagnation. Croatia lost 4.1% of its population during the war (Stipetic 2013: 54). Agriculture, which accounted for 50% of the GDP at the time, was characterised by stability, while the non-agricultural sector was experiencing serious problems. Due to the large number of craftsmen who went to war and to the frontlines, the production and construction activity decreased, and the problem of the lack of raw materials needed to carry out production activities was widespread.

After 1918, Croatia was a part of the newly established state—the Kingdom of Serbs, Croats and Slovenes, later the Kingdom of Yugoslavia. The breakup of Austria–Hungary meant the loss of a large internal market for which the Croatian economy was producing. The new market was narrower, considerably poorer and with a different demand structure (Stipetic 2013: 287). Just like the First World War, the Second World War had left consequences. The war events and occupation have destroyed the Croatian economy. Particularly damaged were the railway lines and a large number of locomotives and wagons, which caused major transport problems in the years that followed (Stipetic 2013: 346).

Since the end of the Second World War until the middle of 1991, the Croatian economy performed depending on the functioning of the unique economic system and the framework of the common development policy of the former Yugoslavia (Sirotkovic 1993: 1). The dominance of the political factor in decision-making on investments and the bureaucratic power represented significant obstacles to the development of entrepreneurship in the then conditions. The Yugoslav workforce was concentrated mainly in large companies and there were almost no companies that had 10–100 employees. Such a structure came about because private companies were being restricted in their scope, either by the maximum number of workers, through tax policy and other measures, while in the social sector, due to the very nature of administrative coordination of economic activity, there was a tendency to form only large companies (Njavro and Franicevic 1990: 177). The consequence of such a ratio between private micro and small companies and large state, that is, public companies is the emergence of the socialist black hole. The socialist "black hole" is the absence of economic units that employ between 10 and 100 workers in the structure of the economies of socialist countries in relation to the economies of Western countries (Njavro and Franicevic 1990: 158).

The fall of the Berlin Wall in 1989 marked the beginning of a new, post-communist era. For the countries of Central, Eastern and South-Eastern Europe, including Croatia, this event marked the beginning of the transition process. In 1991, after the conducted referendum, Croatia proclaimed separation from Yugoslavia and proclaimed sovereignty and independence. This act was met with opposition from Serbia, after which the Serbian aggression and the Homeland War (1991–1995) began. Damage caused by war further worsened the Croatian economic situation and slowed down the transition process. Non-transparent privatisation, which was carried out during the war, was another great problem of the Croatian society. The inherited poor economic structure, political influence on the economy and institutional legacy of communism are the factors that have led to poor implementation of privatisation and created a climate that was unfavourable for the development of entrepreneurship (Haramija and Njavro 2016: 527). Solving the war, transition and privatisation problems neglected the needs of the small and medium-sized enterprise sector, and only in 2002 Croatia has begun to adopt legislation in which small and medium-sized enterprises will find their footing (Kersan-Skabic and Bankovic 2008: 59). The adoption of the Small Business Development Promotion Act was important step, which established the basis for support and development of small and medium-sized enterprises, and the establishment of the Croatian Small Business Agency.

3 Environment for Entrepreneurship

Small and medium enterprises are the backbone of every economy, and their importance is recognised through the share in employment, total revenues and exports. In 2015, there were 106,221 micro, small and medium enterprises (99.7% of the total number of registered enterprises) operating in Croatia, which achieved a share of 54% in total revenues, 69.2% of employment and 50.3% of Croatian exports (Exhibit 1). According to all these three key criteria, small and medium enterprises have increased their share and impact on the economy of Croatia in 2015 in relation to the previous year (Alpeza et al. 2017: 7). Furthermore, it is also significant to mention crafts in the context of entrepreneurship. In 2015, there were 76,222 active crafts in Croatia, which represents 33% of registered business entities. At the end of 2015, active crafts employed 175,942 people (including owners/partners in the crafts and their employees), that is, 13.5% of the total number of employees in legal persons in Croatia (Croatian Chamber of Trades and Crafts 2016).

GEM—Global Entrepreneurship Monitor is the world's largest study of entrepreneurship in which Croatia has been involved since 2002.[2] GEM research monitors the level of activity in starting business ventures measured by the TEA index.[3] Entrepreneurial activity in Croatia measured by the TEA index in 2015 amounts to 7.7%, which is a decline compared to 8% recorded in 2014 and 8.3% in 2013 (Singer et al. 2017). According to this indicator, Croatia slightly lags behind the average of the EU countries (8% in 2015), but significantly lags behind the average of countries whose economies are based on efficiency (to which it belongs), involved in the GEM

---

[2]GEM research in Croatia is carried out by CEPOR—SMEs and Entrepreneurship Policy Center in cooperation with the research team from the Faculty of Economics in Osijek, J.J. Strossmayer University of Osijek.

[3]TEA index represents the number of entrepreneurially active people (it combines the number of people that are trying to start an entrepreneurial venture and the number of owners or owners/managers of enterprises younger than 42 months) per 100 examinees that are 18–64 years old.

Exhibit 1 Small business from Eastern Croatia, producing and exporting bicycle components.
© 2017 BIOS—Business Incubator

research (14.5% in 2015). When analyzing entrepreneurial capacity of a country, it is important to observe differences in motivation for entrepreneurial activity, that is, whether starting an entrepreneurial venture is the result of recognising a business opportunity or lack of other opportunities for employment. GEM research measures starting entrepreneurial ventures because of opportunity or out of necessity using TEA Opportunity, TEA Necessity and motivational index. It is desirable that motivational index is as high as possible, because that speaks of potentially better preparedness for starting a business venture and of greater optimism, which is based on recognised opportunity. Motivational index of Croatia in 2014 and 2015 was just slightly higher than 1 (1.1 in 2014 and 1.5 in 2015), which suggests that the number of entrepreneurs who have started a business venture because of perceived opportunity is almost the same as the number of those who have become entrepreneurs out of necessity (Singer et al. 2017). Croatia has the lowest motivational index of all the EU countries involved in the GEM research and a significantly higher TEA Necessity index than the EU average in the observed period.

The basis for monitoring the dynamics of the small and medium enterprise sector is the data on the establishment of new and closing of existing enterprises. In 2015, there were 14,283 legal entities established in Croatia, which is 7.5% less compared to 2014. According to the results of the GEM research, the rate of exit from business activity, that is, termination of entrepreneurial activity in 2015 in Croatia, was 1.7% and at the level of the EU average (1.9%) (Alpeza et al. 2017: 19). Furthermore, GEM research also monitors the reasons for cessation of business activity. The most common reasons for cessation of business activity in Croatia during 2015 were related to issues of tax policy and administrative burden, followed by problems with access to finance and personal or family reasons.

Women entrepreneurship is an important but still underdeveloped entrepreneurial activity in Croatia. Although the share of women entrepreneurs in Croatia recorded a slight increase in the period from 2010 to 2014, the still present gap in activity of women and men in starting entrepreneurial ventures indicates the consistency of obstacles and insufficient efficiency of programmes and measures for the development and strengthening women entrepreneurship in Croatia. Structural, economic and the so-called soft obstacles have been identified as the key problems of development of women entrepreneurship in Croatia (Strategy of Women Entrepreneurship Development in the Republic of Croatia 2014–2020). The major structural obstacles are stereotypes about women in science and technology, traditional views on the role of women in society and the lack of support for women with two jobs (family and profession). The economic obstacles are related to difficult access to finance and low level of networking of women, while the major "soft" obstacles include lack of advice, mentorship, access to networks of female/male entrepreneurs, training, education and qualification programmes for technologically intensive ventures and lack of self-confidence to take risks. Strategy of Women Entrepreneurship Development in the Republic of Croatia 2014–2020 focuses on removing these obstacles with the aim of increasing the entrepreneurial activity of women and reducing the gap between entrepreneurial start-up activities of women and men.

Croatia is characterised by a well-developed market of bank loans intended for small and medium enterprises. In addition to the offer of their own financial products, commercial banks provide additional lines of financing to entrepreneurs, which are based on business cooperation with ministries, Croatian Bank for Reconstruction and Development, Croatian Agency for SMEs, Innovations and Investments, local self-government units, cities, counties and international financial institutions. Despite this, access to financing for small and medium enterprises in Croatia can be rated as very limited, due to lack of financial resources for the riskier stages of development of entrepreneurial ventures, such as venture capital funds and business angels. Microfinance in Croatia, compared to best international practice, is also underdeveloped, and the following were identified as the main problems: restrictive regulatory framework, inadequate guarantee schemes, inadequate offer of financial products and services (credit unions cannot perform payment transactions, savings are not insured by the Croatian National Bank) and low level of awareness of clients about financial products.

Improving entrepreneurial skills, as one of the priority areas of action aimed at increasing competitiveness of small and medium enterprises, with further implications for the overall economy, has been highlighted by the Government of the Republic of Croatia within the Ministry of Economy, Entrepreneurship and Crafts Strategic Plan for the Period 2015–2017. The said plan emphasises the importance of improving the quality of vocational education, developing entrepreneurial competences, creating stimulating entrepreneurial climate for the growth and development of entrepreneurship, and increasing competitiveness of the Croatian economy.

Exhibit 2 Improving entrepreneurial skills of young, self-employed people. © 2017 BIOS—Business Incubator

Furthermore, the role of lifelong learning is emphasised, as a response to economic problems and increased unemployment, entailing the integration of formal, non-formal and informal learning. Entrepreneurship education has a more significant role at the tertiary level of education than at primary and secondary levels. Students in Croatia are offered the possibility of choosing study programmes in entrepreneurship at undergraduate, graduate and postgraduate levels, university and professional studies at universities, polytechnics and colleges. Furthermore, there is a significant number of institutions in Croatia outside the system of formal education that offer education for beginner entrepreneurs and/or already operational enterprises (Exhibit 2), such as centres for entrepreneurship, business incubators, Croatian Chamber of Economy, Croatian Employers' Association and private enterprises active in the sector of adult education.

Entrepreneurial infrastructure in Croatia comprises of entrepreneurial zones and business support institutions, which include development agencies, centres for entrepreneurship, business incubators (Exhibit 3) and accelerators, business parks, science and technology parks and competence centres.

Their role and criteria for their establishing are described in the Act on Improving Entrepreneurial Infrastructure. The purpose of this Act is to enable start-up and implementation of entrepreneurial activities in standardised conditions of high level of infrastructural equipment within entrepreneurial zones and business support institutions, with the possibility of using a transparent system of incentive measures and benefits. Infrastructure is intended for entrepreneurs in the phase of initial investment and those who are in the phase of expansion of investment activities and operate within the entrepreneurial infrastructure (Exhibit 4).

Exhibit 3 Entrepreneurial incubator BIOS, Osijek, Croatia. © 2017 BIOS—Business Incubator

Exhibit 4 Young self-employed people in business incubator in Croatia. © 2017 BIOS—Business Incubator

4   Towards the Future

The quality of business environment and its impact on the competitiveness of the national economy are the subject of numerous international studies. The studies in which Croatia has been involved in (Global Entrepreneurship Monitor, Doing Business, Global Competitiveness Report, Corruption Perceptions Index) are mutually reinforcing and for many years indicate the continuity of the following obstacles to the development of the small and medium enterprise sector in Croatia (Alpeza et al. 2017):

- Administrative obstacles, especially those related to long and expensive procedures for start-up and termination of enterprises.
- Inefficiency of the judiciary.
- Lengthy ownership registration procedures.
- Inadequacy of educational content for building entrepreneurial competences.
- Underdevelopment of informal forms of financing start-up and growth of business ventures.

The presence of the same obstacles over many years indicates a lack of long-term structural reforms needed to encourage productivity and entrepreneurship in order to initiate economic growth, on which both the standard of citizens and the reduction of unemployment depend.

The analyses of the state of the small and medium enterprise sector needs to be observed on the perspective of achieving the Europe 2020 goals, which is provided by European Semester reports. The European Semester report on the state of the economy in Croatia from 2016[4] state that Croatia came out of its 6 year recession in 2015, with GDP growth of 1.8%. Between 2008 and 2014, real GDP contracted by more than 12%, and the unemployment soared from less than below 9% to more than 17%. The recovery of the economy started at the end of 2014, mostly influenced by the recovery of domestic consumption and to some extent by the investments initiated thanks to the increased absorption of funds from the European Union Funds. The forecast economic growth in the forthcoming period will still not be enough to bring the economy back to pre-recession levels. Strengthening the growth potential requires deep structural reforms in the labour market, interventions in the area of specialisation (which would ensure participation in global value chains), improving productivity and competitiveness (not only through the cost component, but also through improving quality).[5] Without such reforms, Croatia's economy is

---

[4]Communication from the Commission to the European Parliament, the Council, the European Central Bank and the EUROGROUP 2016 European Semester: Assessment of progress on structural reforms, prevention and correction of macroeconomic imbalances and results of in-depth reviews under Regulation (EU) No 1176/2011 {SWD(2016) 71 to SWD(2016) 96} and {SWD (2016) 120}, Brussels, April 07, 2017 COM(2016) 95 final/2.

[5]Commission Staff Working Document Country Report Croatia 2016 Including an In-Depth Review on the prevention and correction of macroeconomic imbalances, Brussels, March 03, 2016 SWD(2016) 80 final/2.

set to return to its long-term potential growth, which is currently estimated at below 1%. Without strengthening the growth potential, the rhythm and intensity of removing macroeconomic imbalances will be slow and insufficient.

From the perspective of achieving the targets of Europe 2020 and the perspective of the European Semester, the development of the Croatian economy, and thus the small and medium enterprise sector in the future period, will depend on the responses to the identified challenges.

5 Case Study: Vitta LTD, Croatia[6]

Introduction

Vitta ltd., an innovative company from Croatia that produces innovative IT solutions for the pharmaceutical industry, is at a crossroads of future development and market positioning. In order to keep its leader position, it needs to make some strategic decisions regarding future product development, target markets (geographically, in terms of customer size and the industry they operate in), and the company's organisational and financial resources.

Company Description

In the beginning, Vitta Ltd. was a supplier of video surveillance equipment, but after some time they have developed a system for monitoring staff attendance, which was a legal requirement in Croatia at the time. Through communication with its largest customer, Vitta Ltd. has recognised the need for development of quality specialised products for the pharmaceutical industry that would allow measurement of temperature and humidity in facilities where pharmaceuticals are stored. After 2 years of development, based on its own resources, Vitta Ltd. started selling its new product VITTO to the customer they were developing it for and later broadened their market and started selling the product to other customers in the pharmaceutical industry. The sales growth and further and constant product and company development were based on rigorous requirements of the pharmaceutical industry for accurate and real-time measurement of humidity and temperature throughout the entire process of storage of medicines.

Product

Today, VITTO is the main product of Vitta Ltd., generating 80% of company's total revenue. Other activities still include video surveillance and the staff attendance monitoring system. Vitta Ltd. has protected the name and its product VITTO in Croatia. The design of names, logos, and promotional materials is exclusively

---

[6]The names of the company and the owner have been changed. However, the presented story and the challenges the company has been facing are real.

The case is prepared by Suncica Oberman Peterka and Mirela Alpeza, Faculty of Economics in Osijek, J.J. Strossmayer University in Osijek, Croatia. Published with the author's permission.

focused on the use of this product in the pharmaceutical industry (production, distribution, sales of pharmaceutical products), although it is possible to customise the product for other industries. The company assembles the final product within its premises. Components come from China, and are sent to the partner in Zagreb, which puts the components together using a CNC machine. The company plans to establish its own accredited calibration laboratory, for which they have already bought parts of the equipment and have invested more than 25,000 euros (they are currently using the services of calibration laboratories in Zagreb and Ljubljana). By establishing their own laboratory, they will be able to provide certification services to other companies. The company's main objective is to manage the entire process: from the manufacture of the product, through its installation at the end user's facility, to regular product maintenance.

The VITTO product is currently at the technological maturity stage of the product life cycle, and it is necessary to work on its improvement, but the company has no available funds to finance development. It was determined that an investment of 10,000 euros was necessary for the improvement and development of a new product. One of the sources of funding should be the profits generated through aggressive sales of VITTO in the next period. The search for alternative sources of financing is quite sporadic. Previous attempts were not successful, which has, together with demanding and time-consuming documentation, further discouraged the company from trying to apply for grants or co-financed funds for innovation.

Organisation of the Company

The owner of the company (Luka) is a computer and electronics technician. His first work experience was in a small company that deals with video surveillance. He found out that he could do a better job, and in 2002 he decided to start his own company with his colleague. They were offering video surveillance services, but they split up after a while, and Luka established Vitta Ltd., together with another colleague. In 2007, they decided to part ways, and Luka finally started to work independently with three employees who decided to stay with him. They are still employees of the Vitta Ltd. company. The company today has ten employees. When employing people, Luka is looking for young, bright people who are willing to work and learn new things. Since this is a specific industry, the character of the person and the willingness to learn and work are of particular importance. The company compensates its employees with a fixed salary and incentives, which are determined by the company's owner and manager on a monthly basis. The owner of the company believes that all employees are important and that it would be really hard to find a replacement for any of them. They are the main resource of the company. In 2015, the company moved to new premises with new offices, warehouse, laboratory and future laboratory for calibration of probes and common areas.

Market

The majority of pharmacies (about 300 pharmacies) in Croatia are already users of the VITTO product and thus customers of Vitta Ltd. Luka and his closest employees believe that it is time to broaden their market to pharmaceutical wholesalers. They have already contacted the Croatian Chamber of Pharmacists and informed them about the product they offer, so the Chamber could recommend them as a supplier that has a product that meets the legal regulations within the industry. Furthermore, in cooperation with the Croatian Chamber of Pharmacists, they have organised a training course where they have presented VITTO to potential customers. The limiting factor for greater penetration of the pharmacy market is insufficiently clearly and firmly defined legislation, as well as currently very flexible monitoring of compliance with legislation by inspectors. There are several competitors in Croatia that offer similar, but technologically less advanced products.

Currently, the biggest challenge for the company is the entry into foreign markets, but they have yet to solve the issue of technical support and equipment installation in foreign markets. They plan to further simplify the device and produce a "kit" allowing self-installation of the device.

Challenges for the Company
The owner of the company is satisfied with development of the VITTO product that meets the criteria of demanding legislative regulations in the pharmaceutical industry. At the same time, the company is aware that they need to constantly develop and innovate their products and services and they are considering two possible alternatives: entering foreign markets with the existing product with improved technological performances (self-installation kit) and offering similar products with the capability to measure other parameters in other industries to new customers.

Although the superior market position of VITTO in Croatia in terms of technology, compared to the competition, is evident, its market potential is only partially exploited (15/200 wholesalers and 300/1000 pharmacies).

Considering the fact that VITTO has reached the stage of maturity in the product life cycle (in the technological sense), there is pressure to maximise profits from sales and generate resources for further development, which requires investing considerable effort into sales.

References

Alpeza, M., Has, M., Novosel, M., & Singer, S. (2017). *Small and medium enterprises report – Croatia 2016 including the results of GEM – Global entrepreneurship monitor research for Croatia for 2015*. Zagreb: CEPOR - SMEs and Entrepreneurship Policy Centre.

Croatian Bureau of Statistic. (2016). *Statistical yearbook of the Republic of Croatia*. Zagreb: Croatian Bureau of Statistic.

Haramija, P., & Njavro, D. (2016). Tranzicija i njezini rezultati – zasto tranzicija iz komunistickog u demokratski sustav trzisnog gospodarstva nije ostvarila ocekivanja. *Obnovljeni zivot: casopis za filozofiju i religijske znanosti, 71*(4), 515–527.

Horbec, I. (2013). *Habsburska Monarhija u potrazi za mirom i blagostanjem. Hrvatske zemlje u 18. stoljecu*. Zagreb: Ur. L. Coralic, Matica Hrvatska.

Hrvatska obrtnicka komora. (2016). *Obrtnistvo u brojkama*. Zagreb: Hrvatska obrtnicka komora.

Kersan-Skabic, I., & Bankovic, M. (2008). Malo gospodarstvo u Hrvatskoj i ulazak u Europsku uniju. *Ekonomska misao i praksa, 1*(1), 57–75.

Ministarstvo poduzetnistva i obrta. (2014a). *Strategija razvoja poduzetništva zena u Republici Hrvatskoj 2014–2020*. Zagreb: Ministarstvo poduzetnistva i obrta.

Ministarstvo poduzetnistva i obrta. (2014b). *Strateski plan Ministarstva poduzetnistva i obrta za razdoblje 2015–2017*. Zagreb: Ministarstvo poduzetnistva i obrta.

Njavro, D., & Franicevic, V. (1990). *Poduzetništvo – Teorija, Politika, Praksa*. Zagreb: Privredni vjesnik.

Singer, S., Sarlija, N., Pfeifer, S., & Oberman Peterka, S. (2017). *Sto cini Hrvatsku (ne) poduzetnickom zemljom? GEM Hrvatska 2016*. Zagreb: CEPOR – SMEs and Entrepreneurship Policy Centre.

Sirotkovic, J. (1993). *Hrvatsko gospodarstvo 1945–1992 Ekonomski uzroci sloma Jugoslavije i oruzane agresije na Hrvatsku*. Zagreb: Hrvatska akademija znanosti i umjetnosti.

Skrtic, M. (2006). *Poduzetnistvo*. Zagreb: Sinergija nakladništvo.

Stipetic, V. (2001). *Povijest hrvatske ekonomske misli (1298–1847)*. Zagreb: Golden Marketing.

Stipetic, V. (2013). *Povijest hrvatske ekonomske misli (1848–1968)*. Zagreb: Sveuciliste u Zagrebu –Ekonomski fakultet.

Mirela Alpeza is an Associate Professor at the J.J. Strossmayer University of Osijek, Croatia where she teaches courses on SME Business Transfer, Family Entrepreneurship, Corporate Entrepreneurship and Competitive Intelligence. Since 2011, she is the director of CEPOR—SMEs & Entrepreneurship Policy Center in Zagreb. Her main fields of interest are sustainability of SMEs in business transfer processes, family entrepreneurship and takeover entrepreneurship. She has established the Center for Family Business and Business Transfer, aimed at supporting SMEs in coping with business transfer challenges. In 2015 she conducted the Business Transfer Barometer research and provided policy recommendations for development of business transfer ecosystem in Croatia. She is a member of the European Council for Small Business and Entrepreneurship (Vice-President for Croatia).

Suncica Oberman Peterka is an Associate Professor at the J.J. Strossmayer University of Osijek, Faculty of Economics in Osijek, where she teaches different courses on Entrepreneurship, New Venture Creation, Strategic Management and Leadership, at undergraduate, graduate, and postgraduate levels. Since 2012, she is the head of undergraduate and graduate educational program in Entrepreneurship and since October 2013, she holds the position of Vice-Dean, responsible for students and educational programmes. She is a member of the International Council for Small Business, the European Council for Small Business, and the Croatian Association of Economists, and she is one of the founders of the ALUMNI association of the Faculty of Economics in Osijek.

Maja Has is a PhD student at the Faculty of Economics and Business, University of Zagreb, Croatia. She completed her Master's degree in Analysis and Business planning at the Faculty of Economics and Business, University of Zagreb. She is employed as an Assistant Accountant at Kit Biro Ltd., Zagreb, and an External Associate at CEPOR—SMEs & Entrepreneurship Policy Center. Her areas of interest are entrepreneurship, development of the SME sector, SME accounting, and management accounting.

Entrepreneurship in Kosovo

Muhamet Mustafa and Besnik A. Krasniqi

Abstract Kosovo is the newest country in Europe located in the central Balkan Peninsula. Kosovo is a lower-middle-income economy and has experienced solid economic growth over the last decade. It has experienced growth every year since the onset of the global financial crisis in 2008. The most economic development has taken place in the trade, services, retail, and construction sectors. Kosovo is highly dependent on remittances from the Diaspora, FDI, and other capital inflows. The country provides opportunities for growth in tourism, manufacturing and high value-added services being most promising for growth.

1 Introduction

Kosovo (Albanian: Kosova) is a small landlocked country in South-eastern Europe, in the centre of Balkan Peninsula, formerly an constituent part of Yugoslavia with an area of 10,908 km^2. Prishtina (Exhibit 1) is the capital of Republic of Kosovo. It is one of the smallest countries in Europe and is the newest country in Europe (Exhibit 2). It is situated in South-Eastern Europe bordering Albania to the south-west, Montenegro to northwest, Serbia to northeast, and Macedonia to the south (KAS, Statistical Yearbook 2017).

M. Mustafa
Riinvest College, Prishtina, Kosovo
e-mail: muhamet.mustafa@riinvestinstitute.org

B. A. Krasniqi (✉)
University of Prishtina "Hasan Prishtina", Prishtina, Kosovo
e-mail: besnik.krasniqi@uni-pr.edu

© Springer International Publishing AG, part of Springer Nature 2018
R. Palalić et al. (eds.), *Entrepreneurship in Former Yugoslavia*,
https://doi.org/10.1007/978-3-319-77634-7_4

Exhibit 1 Prishtina, the capital city. © 2017 Besnik A. Krasniqi

Exhibit 2 The NEWBORN Monument in the capital city of Prishtina. © 2017 Besnik A. Krasniqi

Table 1 Languages and
native speakers in Kosovo

Language	Native speakers	%
Albanian	1,644,865	94.5
Bosnian	28,989	1.7
Serbian	27,983	1.6
Turkish	19,568	1.1
Romani	5860	0.3
Other/not specified	12,560	0.7

1.1 Demographics

- Population: 1,739,825 (2011 Census). Resident population for 2016 (31 Dec 2016) was 1.783.531 (KAS, Statistical Yearbook of Kosovo 2017)
- Ethnic groups: Albanians 91.0%, Serb 3.4%, others 5.6% (Bosnian, Turks, Roma, Ashkali, Egyptians, Goran, and others (2011 census and estimation in 2015)
- Languages based on Kosovo's Census 2011 ("Language in Kosovo". Kosovo Agency of Statistics (KAS). Archived from the original on 2015-02-17) are indicated in Table 1.
- Religions: Muslim 85.6%, Catholic 5%, Orthodox 10%, others 0.06%, none 0.10%, not stated 0.55%. (Kosovo Agency of Statistics (KAS). Ask.rks-gov. net. 2011. Retrieved 2017-08-29)

2 Historical Overview

The Kosovo lands were part of Dardania and Illyria in ancient times (Exhibit 3). Later the territory of today's province was for centuries ruled by the Ottoman Empire. After World War II, Kosovo became an autonomous province of the former Yugoslavia, which though communist, distanced itself from Moscow's rule. Dissatisfied with the exercise of power by the majority Serbs and occupation from Serbia during 1990s, the Kosovar Albanians succeeded in establishing their freedom in 1999 after the War against Serbia with support of NATO and won its independence in 2008.

Kosovo has developed ties to Western Europe and especially USA, which has assisted Kosovo's transformation to a market economy with final aim to become part of EU. In 2002, Kosovo has adopted Euro. The flag displays six white stars in an arc above a golden map of Kosovo on a blue field. They are officially meant to symbolise Kosovo's six major ethnic groups: Albanians, Serbs, Turks, Gorani, Roma, and Bosniaks (Exhibit 4).

Exhibit 3 Goddess on the Throne is one of the most precious archaeological artefacts of Kosovo and has been adopted as the symbol of Prishtina. It dates back to 3500 BC in the Neolithic period and is made of clay. MKRS, Guidë arkeologjike e Kosovës (2012)

Exhibit 4 The flag of Kosovo

3 Environment for Entrepreneurship

3.1 Economy

The World Bank (2017a) reported the Gross Domestic Product (GDP) in Kosovo was worth US$6.65 billion in 2016. The GDP value of Kosovo represents 0.01% of the world economy. GDP in Kosovo averaged US$4.98 billion from 2000 until 2016, reaching an all-time high of US$7.39 billion in 2014 and a record low of US

$1.85 billion in 2000. Kosovo was the poorest region with the lowest level of GDP per capita, originating from heavy metal and mineral extraction industries associated with production of unfinished goods. The structure of Kosovan economy during former Yugoslavia was mainly driven by the needs of other republics. The development of large socially owned enterprises was encouraged by the natural endowment of Kosovo and the needs of Serbia and other parts of Yugoslavia for raw materials and unfinished goods mainly metal-based products (Krasniqi 2010, 2012a). Kosovo had the highest share of employment in the large social sector enterprises (those with over 1000 employees), suggesting that Kosovo had an unbalanced economic structure mainly based on extraction industries.

The Kosovo's transitional path from centrally planned to a market economy, interrupted by conflict, occupation, and war (1998–1999), has influenced the economic development of the country. Kosovo is amongst poorest European countries with GDP per capita of 2800 Euros generated from services (56%), industry 18%, agriculture 17%, and construction 10%. (EU 2014). Deindustrialisation marked by the shrink of industry share of GDP (47% 1989 to 15% during early stage of the post conflict period) influenced heavy imbalances in macroeconomic configuration. Trade deficit reaching about 40% of GDP and unemployment rate above 30% are key problems. On the other side, macroeconomic and fiscal stability and low inflation persisted along with modest economic growth 2–4%. The remittances (about 14% of GDP) and donor contribution, especially during the emergent reconstruction phase, fueled the development of SMEs by generating high aggregate demand. In terms of the institutional environment, aftermath of the War, Kosovo had to start everything from the scratch (Krasniqi 2012a): from a business environment without legislation in place at all to a country which has progressed much in adopting its legislation with EU laws. Although the legal framework is almost completed and in compliance with EU standards, implementation and weak rule of law remains a severe problem for entrepreneurship development.

Recent surveys report that the unfair competition, corruption, and rule of law hinders the general environment of doing business. High corruption practices of public officials and inherited tradition of parallel system during the occupation created special forms of business practices—doing business partially or fully informal.[1] According to the most recent survey, the informal sector is estimated to be around 35% (Riinvest 2013). Under these circumstances, this environment created incentives for emerging strong normative or informal social institutions, which acted as a complementary to formal institutions or in some areas replaced them (Dana 2010; Krasniqi and Mustafa 2016). Experiences of entrepreneurs during the

---

[1]Note that during the communism, small firm sector was underdeveloped in Montenegro, Macedonia, and in the southern province of Kosovo, though in Kosovo, a very large ethnic Albanian-based informal sector, compensated for the deficit of formal (i.e. registered) small enterprises Bateman (2000) Small Enterprise Development in the Ygoslav Successor States: Institutions and Institutional Development in a Post-War Environment. *MOST: Economic Policy in Transitional Economies* 10: 171–206.

communist era and during the occupation period from Serbia rooted these practices in social lives. The entrepreneurship took the form of parallel or informal activity.

3.2   Entrepreneurship and SMEs Sector

The roots of private enterprises in Kosovo can be found in ancient times. Before the Second World War, the private sector in Kosovo consisted of family businesses concentrated mostly in agriculture, cattle raising, and handicrafts under poor conditions and using relatively primitive technology. Producers of basic consumption goods, traditional artisans, and small manufacturers dominated the production activities, while the service sector consisted of traditional services such as carpenters, leather craftsman, and blacksmiths. In the trade sector, there was a small group of merchants who operated no further than neighbouring countries (Riinvest 1998; Krasniqi 2012a; Ramadani and Dana 2013).

During the phase of the centralised socialist system (1945–1950),[2] Kosovo's private economy was limited to family farms (in agriculture), greengrocers, small shops, restaurants, tailors, and handicrafts. In 1950, the Soviet type socialism was abandoned, and the economic system was modified towards a more market-oriented system or the so-called self-management socialism. Although changes in the institutional environment permitted the establishment of small private enterprises, the growth of private firms was legally restricted. Private firms were limited by the number of employees they could hire and in agriculture by the area of land that could be owned by private farm owners.[3] Institutional constraints to private sector growth during this period resulted in a limited number of small shops, handicrafts and only slightly more in agriculture. Moreover, because of its political status, Kosovo (i.e. centralised administration of Kosovo which was under Serbia) was not allowed to devise its autonomous economic policies before 1974. During that period, Kosovo was the most underdeveloped region of former Yugoslavia. In 1974, with the new Constitution, Kosovo was given a substantial degree of autonomy including the management of its own economy and was put in an almost equal position with other seven federal units.[4]

---

[2]Broadly speaking, Yugoslav socialism can be divided into three phases: 1945–1950, 1951–1974, and 1974–1989.

[3]The number of employees was limited to 10, and the size of plots owned by private entities in agriculture was limited to 10 ha.

[4]Even in 1969, Kosovo was recognised as a territorial unit in its own right and with a Constitutional Law on Kosovo. In 1974, Kosovo was formally recognised as an autonomous province. The new constitution in 1974 effectively gave quasi-independence to the Republics and autonomy status for two regions in Serbia, Kosovo, and Vojvodina. Each Republic and both autonomous provinces were henceforth able (at least in theory) to articulate an almost fully independent monetary and fiscal policy, each having its own "central bank" and each being able to jealously guard its enterprise sector through financial means and restrictions on trade (Pleština 1992).

Within the former Yugoslavia, development of the small enterprise sector had a pronounced regional bias. The small firm sector was very well developed in the northern province of Vojvodina, more or less comparable to Slovenia and Croatia. Notwithstanding, this sector was underdeveloped in Montenegro, Macedonia, and in the southern province of Kosovo, though in Kosovo, a very large ethnic Albanian-based informal sector compensated for the deficit of formal (i.e. registered) small enterprises (Bateman 2000).

Until the 1980s, the average number of employees in the private sector remained well below the legal limit of five employees in all parts of former Yugoslavia. In 1970, the average number of employees in small private enterprises was only 1.5 (Reljin 1988, p. 80). This figure was even lower as a result of the growing economic crisis which stimulated a wave of individuals entering self-employment in the late 1970s and early 1980s (Bateman 2000). Even after the removal of the remaining formal legal restrictions on hired employees and other formal entry and growth barriers in the late 1970s, during the period of 1981–1991, the average number of employees only went up to 2.5 employees (Bartlett 1990, p. 95). Despite the low level of economic development compared to other parts of former Yugoslavia, the existence of small private firms in Kosovo during socialism, although limited, had positive influences on the successful start of the development of private initiatives and entrepreneurship in the period after 1989 (Krasniqi and Mustafa 2016). In particular, it is worth mentioning that the political position of Albanians under the former Yugoslavia contributed to a more positive and proactive approach to the political reforms, which led to a breakup of Yugoslavia.

In 1989, the federal government of Yugoslavia launched a large package of economic reforms in order to stabilise the economy, fight hyperinflation, and establish a market economy. Under this new legislation, all restrictions on the formation of private enterprise were removed.[5] In response to these changes, the number of private businesses in Kosovo increased rapidly as everywhere else in TEs. However, the process of economic reforms and hence small firm development was interrupted by political circumstances and events of that period, particularly those associated with the "emergency rule" and occupation by the Serbian regime and the breakup of Yugoslavia.

In 1990, the Serbian government forcefully suppressed the autonomy of Kosovo, abolished all institutions of self-government, imposed emergency rule in Kosovo, and shifted the decision-making power to the Serbian Parliament and government. As a result of the "emergency rule", about 70% (150,000) of the Albanian employees of the public/state sector, and other legal social and cultural institutions, were dismissed from their jobs by force (Riinvest 1998).

In order to secure the survival of themselves and their families, many ethnic Albanian citizens established their own enterprises. Thus, the main factor contributing to the establishment of private small businesses was the so-called push factor,

---

[5]Službeni List SFRJ, Zakon o Produzčama, br. 77/88, 40/89, 46/90, 61/90. (Official Gazette of Federal Republic of Yugoslavia, Law on Enterprises, no 77/88, 40/89, 46/90, 61/90).

while the "pull", regarded as a demand-driven motive, had only a minor impact (Krasniqi 2014). Firstly, during the communist era, Albanians were discriminated in the labour market and, secondly, the massive dismissal of social-public sector workers at the beginning of 1990 had a tremendous impact on incentives for business start-ups.

The significant growth in the number of new businesses took place between 1991 and 1993 when the number of private firms tripled. This period of the rapid growth was followed by a period of stagnation as perhaps the social and political conditions deteriorated and declined in 1998, when the occupation started to manifest in its extreme form (Krasniqi 2007). Government authorities imposed arbitrary fines and penalties on Albanian businesses, inflicted violence and finally war. The slowdown of the private sector during that time was reflected in the fall of output too. The evidence suggests that in 1995 output in the economy decreased drastically to half of that in 1989 (Riinvest 1998). Although the data for period of 1997–1999 is not available, it is believed that the situation in terms of SME development did not improve due to the rising level of ethnic tensions and eventually the war.

3.3 Development of Entrepreneurship in Kosovo After the War

In the aftermath of the War, the second sharp increase in the number of business start-ups took place. The total number of register business in 2003 was 49,874 and experienced huge increase thereafter by reaching 159,724 in 2016 (Agency for Business Registration 2017). Majority of private companies are SMEs suggesting that private sector consists entirely of small firms (Krasniqi and Mustafa 2016; Krasniqi 2014; Lajqi and Krasniqi 2017).

On the type of business ownership, majority of businesses are organised as individual businesses. According to the Agency for Business Registration (ABR) in 2016, 85% of enterprises were registered as individual. Based on data from the same sources, there is a significant change in terms of legal format of businesses in the recent years. We have a decrease in number of individual businesses while we have increase in business partnerships and limited liability companies. From the total number of registered businesses (159,724), 85.22% are registered as individual businesses, 2.44% as general partnerships, and 11.28% as limited liability companies. Compared to 2003, the number of foreign owned companies has increased significantly by 0.5%, suggesting more active role of foreign companies in Kosovo.

Another feature of the private sector of Kosovo is dominance of firms in trade and services sector compared to other sectors especially manufacturing. The number of production companies has remained very low since 2000 with slow increase in the recent years. Although slow, percentage share of production companies has increased from 4.9% in 2008 to 6.35% in 2014, which shows an improvement in terms of production sector. According to KPMG (2017), the added value from manufacturing sectors in the country remained low during 2015; thus, the country's economy continued to face imbalances against the external sector. The growth in internal demand went on to further increase imports which translated into the increase of current account deficit.

This is important, having a significant impact on exports. The growth of this sector will have significant effect in improving trade deficit in Kosovo. The private sector in Kosovo generates 145,736 jobs in 2014. Accordingly, the trade sectors provide 37% of jobs in private sector and is followed by manufacturing which shares 15.3%, construction 9.1%, and hotels 7.2%.

3.4 Business Environment and Entrepreneurship

The dynamic growth of the new private sector has been one of the key driving forces behind the economic recovery in all former communist countries. Despite its importance, the business environment has not been very conducive for SMEs. Institutions and their quality are key determinants of private sector development. The findings of the Riinvest SME surveys suggest that Kosovo is not an exception either (Riinvest 2001–2004). However, unlike other TEs, Kosovo faced specific challenges in building market economy institutions. Because of the War, the transformation process and privatisation was delayed while new institutions were built from scratch. One of the main challenges in this transition path was the creation of new institutions and favourable business environment for entrepreneurship. Based on the experiences of other TEs, the promotion of entrepreneurship and small firms remains the single solution to promote economic development (Krasniqi 2007, 2009). Despite their importance, SMEs in Kosovo still face an unfriendly business environment.

Riinvest Survey results in various years show that in Aftermath of the War, entrepreneurs are more concerned with constraints related to the external environment rather than with internal factors such as managerial or employees' skills, which were ranked at the very bottom of the list of constraints. The presence of an informal economy and corruption, which in turn is affected by an inadequate legal framework, creates an uncompetitive business environment, leading to the increased cost of doing business for firms that operate officially compared to their counterparts that operate informally or partially informally. The interesting conclusion emerges from the ranking and comparisons of the business obstacles into two categories: external and internal business environment obstacles. It is clear that the external environment is considered by entrepreneurs to be far more important for small firm development compared to internal factors such as the availability of skilled labour and that of both employees and managers which scored lowest in the list of obstacles. One question that may arise is whether small firms have access to sufficient skilled human capital or maybe human capital is not a key element for them (even if we assume that they have access to skilled human capital) compared to external environment obstacles which have the key role in their business (Krasniqi 2012b).

Exhibit 5 Rugova Canyon. © 2017 Besnik A. Krasniqi

However, in recent years, Kosovo has significantly improved its business regulations as captured by the Doing Business indicators, which shows the country is implementing reforms to narrow the gap with the global regulatory frontier (World Bank 2017b). Doing Business 2017 finds that Kosovo made paying taxes easier by introducing an online system for filing and paying VAT and social security contributions. Nowadays, paying taxes is less costly by allowing more types of expenses to be deducted for the calculation of corporate income tax. In addition, Kosovo also made trading across borders easier by reducing the time and cost of documentary compliance and the time of border compliance for exporting by improving its automated customs data management system, streamlining customs clearance processes, and implementing the Albania–Kosovo Transit Corridor.

3.5 *Rugova Canyon and Brezovica Resort*

The mountains in Kosovo offer good opportunities for winter tourism, and the most prominent sites are the Brezovica and Rugova, which are distinguished as skiing and recreational centres. Rugova Canyon (Exhibit 5) and Brezovica Resort (Exhibit 6) are one of the major touristic destinations for mountain tourism. Both touristic destinations offer a great opportunity for investors especially foreign investors as they are in the process of restructuring and looking forward to attracting strategic investors. As such they will offer as an important source of income for local economy.

Exhibit 6 Brezovica Mountains. © 2017 Besnik A. Krasniqi

The numerous landscapes and other tourist attractions, two of the most prominent being the Rugova Canyon and the Gadime Cave, make Kosovo a destination worth visiting.

4 Toward the Future

The future of Kosovo seems to be bright in terms of integration in European Union which will enable Kosovo more entrepreneurial opportunities. Kosovo already has adopted the Euro currency in 1 January 2002, which has considerable increased the cost of goods and services in the country. The Kosovo offers still numerous opportunities with privatisation process which is not completed yet.

The geographic location of Kosovo allows entrepreneurs to grow their ventures in surrounding countries. Kosovo has very good infrastructural connection with Albania and its main Port in Durres, Serbia, Macedonia, Bulgaria, and Turkey. Kosovo has already signed bilateral agreement and benefits from preferential treatment of goods and services from Kosovo exported to EU. In aftermath of the War in Kosovo, there was a high donor activity in supporting reconstruction of Kosovo. Currently, Kosovo benefits a lot from donor programs in area of entrepreneurship training. EU and USA have contributed a lot in terms of educational system by providing a lot of youth with educational opportunities abroad. These graduates may be found in various managerial positons in private companies and organisations and form a human capital which, although limited, could be available for foreign investors. To this end, the donors have contributed in the form of start-up capital in the country to form and grow ventures as well as incubator facilities available especially in ICT sector which is becoming promising for growth. In addition, some other sectors such as mining, wood processing, agriculture, energy, and construction capital city present good investment opportunities to take advantage of the young population, the growing economy, and the fairly untapped natural resources of the country. To promote these opportunities, recently, the Assembly of the Republic of Kosovo has adopted Law on Strategic Investments in the Republic of Kosovo to facilitate, attract, and create the necessary conditions to make entrepreneurial opportunities in Kosovo, attractive to international investors.

5   Hymeri Kleemann Company L.L.C.: Opportunity-Driven Entrepreneur

Company Background

Hymeri Kleemann LCC. (HK) was established on September 2007 in Prishtina, Kosovo, with the vision to be a specialised company in the segment of elevators and escalators in Kosovo's Market. The founder is a young and dynamic person, well-educated holding master's degree in management from a reputable European university. Before moving to entrepreneurial career, he was working for a foreign bank in Kosovo, where he held various managerial positions for more than 8 years. Despite good managerial position and well-paid job, he decided to move into entrepreneurial career.

As of March 2009, HK after a professional and trustful cooperation with the Kleemann Manufacturer became an authorised and exclusive partner of Kleemann Group for the territory of Kosovo market and therefore named as Hymeri Kleemann LLC. During last 7 years, HK operates with its business activity in segment of Projecting, Sales, Installation, and Service & Maintenance of different models of elevators and escalators in Kosovo market. Furthermore, since November 2009, HK started its business activity in Albanian market as well.

Business Expansion Strategy

HK's Vision and Mission is driven by mission statement "Your Trust, Our Responsibility…"; Safety & health, customer focus, social and environmental responsibility are the main drivers towards our reputation and success. HK adds values to all stakeholders by providing quality, professional services, and products through our highly organised and efficient teams. By being honourable, innovative, and responsive, we will be the most preferred service provider in the industry.

The owner of HK is opportunity-driven entrepreneur. Since October 2009, HK has expanded its business activity in the Albanian market as well. Recently, HK has established its own company in Germany and has made first sales into EU market, mainly Germany, with the possibility of expansion in Austria, France, and elsewhere.

Diversification

After a great success in the field of elevators and escalators, as well as a high number of requests from various residents, in 2011 Hymeri Kleemann established a subsidiary named HY-ECO. HY-ECO is a provider of integrated property maintenance services offering professional cleaning of building complexes, allocated electricity payment for the common areas of the building including elevator electricity expense, camera monitoring services, and home repair services. Since the company's services are defined by the quality of its staff, the company ensures that all the members of its teams are trained in the industry's best practices, with friendly, professional, and reliable attitudes, and are committed to customer care. The provision of top quality services, correctness in the services offered, as well as the regular monthly maintenance of the building complexes have led the company to acquire a relatively satisfactory share in the market for a relatively short period of time. For the time being, the company offers its maintenance services in 120 residential buildings in Prishtina. Due to satisfactory services provided by HY-ECO, there have been many requests from home residents to start providing a wider range of services within home repair services. Therefore, in October 2014, HY-ECO has established a new brand named Mjeshtri for the required services mentioned above. The expansion of the company is clearly shown in Table 2.

Table 2 Milestones

September 2007	Registration of company Hymeri LLC in Kosovo with activities: Projecting, Sales, Installation, and Service & Maintenance of different models of elevators and escalators
March 2008	First import of elevators in Kosovo
March 2009	Hymeri LLC became an authorised and exclusive partner of Kleemann group for the territory of Kosovo market and, therefore, named as Hymeri Kleemann LLC.
October 2009	Registration of company Hymeri LLC in Albania
October 2011	Hymeri Kleemann established a subsidiary named HY-ECO
December 2011	Signing contracts with QKUK for repair and maintenance of 43 elevators (lifts of all hospitals in Prishtina)
March 2012	Signing contracts with QKUK for continued maintenance of 43 elevators (lifts of all hospitals in Prishtina)
November 2012	Registration of company HY-ECO LLC in Kosovo with activities: Maintenance of water installation, maintenance of installation of electricity, maintenance of installation of heating and repairs)
October 2014	HY-ECO has established a new brand named "Mjeshtri"
December 2014	Super brands award winner Kosovo's choice 2014/2015
March 2015	Hymeri Kleemann LLC certified by TUV Austria with management system EN ISO 9001:2008 for sales, installation, maintenance, and servicing of elevators and escalators
2017	Started operation in Germany

Expansion to European Market

In terms of international market, HK started to operate in Germany and has a clear vision to become sustainable business in European market. With its clear strategy formulation, HK aims to become direct contractor of large scale construction companies in the EU market. HK has difficult task in supporting its expansion into foreign markets. It has challenges in terms of identifying an effective practice of recruiting and keeping highly skilled employees at the time of increasing international demand for its services. The pool of talent in Kosovo is limited so far in terms of skilled employees. Thus, the lack of qualified labour in Kosovo market is one of the biggest challenges to meet its increasing demand for its services. In addition, this is another problem to consider expansion to another market segment such as businesses as well as expansion in regional and European markets. HK is considering innovative ways of establishing an internationally recognised training centre to support its growth to international market.

References

Agency for Business Registration. (2017). *Business register*. Prishtina: Agency for Business Registration.

Bartlett, W. (1990). Discrimination and ethnic tension in Yugoslavia: The case of Kosovo. In M. Wyzan (Ed.), *The political economy of ethnic discrimination and affirmative action: A comprehensive perspective* (pp. 197–216). New York: Praeger.

Bateman, M. (2000). Small enterprise development in the Yugoslav successor states: Institutions and institutional development in a post-war environment. *MOST: Economic Policy in Transitional Economies, 10*(2), 171–206.

Dana, L.-P. (2010). *When economies change hands: A survey of entrepreneurship in the emerging markets of Europe from the Balkans to the Baltic states*. Oxford: Routledge.

EU Commission. (2014). Staff working document: Kosovo 2014 progress report, Brussels, 2014.

KAS. (2011). *Kosovo census 2011*. Prishtina: Kosovo Agency of Statistics.

KAS. (2017). *Statistical yearbook*. Prishtina: Kosovo Agency of Statistics.

KPMG. (2017). *Investment in Kosovo 2017*. Prishtina: KPMG Albania Shpk Kosovo Branch.

Krasniqi, B. A. (2007). Barriers to entrepreneurship and SME growth in transition: The case of Kosova. *Journal of Developmental Entrepreneurship, 12*(01), 71–94.

Krasniqi, B. A. (2009). Personal, household and business environmental determinants of entrepreneurship. *Journal of Small Business and Enterprise Development, 16*(1), 146–166.

Krasniqi, B. A. (2010). *Determinants of entrepreneurship and small business growth in transition economies: The case of Kosova*. Doctoral dissertation, Stoke-on-Trent, UK: Staffordshire University.

Krasniqi, B. A. (2012a). *Entrepreneurship and small business development in Kosova*. New York: Nova Science Publishers.

Krasniqi, B. A. (2012b). Building an expanded small firm growth model in a transitional economy: Evidence on fast growing firms. *Journal of East-West Business, 18*(3), 231–273.

Krasniqi, B. A. (2014). Characteristics of self-employment: A refuge from unemployment or road to entrepreneurship. *Small Enterprise Research, 21*(1), 33–53.

Krasniqi, B. A., & Mustafa, M. (2016). Small firm growth in a post-conflict environment: The role of human capital, institutional quality, and managerial capacities. *International Entrepreneurship and Management Journal, 12*(4), 1165–1207.

Lajqi, S., & Krasniqi, B. A. (2017). Entrepreneurial growth aspirations in challenging environment: The role of institutional quality, human and social capital. *Strategic Change, 26*(4), 385–401.

MKRS. (2012). *Guidë arkeologjike e Kosovës*. Prishtine: Minsitria e Kulturës, Rinisë dhe Sporteve.

Pleština, D. (1992). *Regional development in communist Yugoslavia: Success failure and consequences*. Boulder: Westview Press.

Ramadani, V., & Dana, L. P. (2013). The state of entrepreneurship in the Balkans: Evidence from selected countries. In V. Ramadani & R. C. Schneider (Eds.), *Entrepreneurship in the Balkans* (pp. 217–250). Heidelberg: Springer.

Reljin, S. (1988). *Mala privreda u agrokompleksu (the small firm sector in Agrocomplexes)*. Proceedings of the First Symposium on the Small Firm Sector Today, Centre for Small Enterprise Development, Braca Karic Enterprise, Peč, Yugoslavia.

Riinvest. (1998). *Economic activities and democratic development of Kosova*. Prishtinë: Riinvest Institute for Development Research.

Riinvest. (2013). *A business perspective on informality in Kosova, research report*. Prishtine: Riinvest Institute for Development Research.

Riinvest. (various years). *SME development in Kosova*. Prishtinë: Riinvest Institute for Development Research.

Službeni List SFRJ, Zakon o produzečama, br 77/88, 40/89, 46/90, 61/90. (Official Gazette of Federal Republic of Yugoslavia, Law on Enterprises, no 77/88, 40/89, 46/90, 61/90).

World Bank. (2017a). *World Bank indicators – Kosovo*. Washington, DC: World Bank.

World Bank. (2017b). *World Bank doing business 2016*. Washington, DC: World Bank.

Muhamet Mustafa is the former President and founder of Riinvest Institute in Kosovo (Kosova). He was Minister-coordinator for the Economic Development and Planning in the Government of former Yugoslavia (1986–1989), Minister for Development of Kosovo's government (1984–1986), and Director of the Fund for Road Construction in Kosovo (1981–1984). He has also served as a Member of Parliament in the Assembly of the Republic of Kosovo. Dr. Mustafa is the author of numerous papers published in various professional and scientific journals and presented in symposiums and conferences, as well as several books: Income Policy and Productivity (1981), Organization of the Investment System and the Economic Development of Kosovo (1985), Cybernetics in Economy (1989, 1990), Cybernetics and Introduction to Informatics (1995), Management of Investment Projects (1997), Investment Management (2004), and Small and Medium Business Development (2006). Dr. Mustafa is also a co-founder of the Riinvest University and a professor at Faculty of Economics in University of Prishtina.

Besnik A. Krasniqi a Fulbright Postdoctoral Scholar, holds MA and PhD in Economics from Staffordshire University (UK). He teaches Small Business and Entrepreneurship, Innovation Management, and Research Methods at University of Prishtina in graduate and postgraduate studies. His professional career spans teaching and research in entrepreneurship at Maastricht School of Management (the Netherlands), Indiana University (USA) and University of Michigan (USA), Staffordshire University (UK), State University of Tetovo (Macedonia), and Riinvest Institute for Development Research (Kosovo). He has authored several books, numerous research reports, and consultancy assignments. His research work in the area of entrepreneurship, firm growth, institutions, SME finance, informal economy, and transition and emerging economies appeared in international journals such as Small Business Economics, International Entrepreneurship and Management Journal, and Economic Systems.

Entrepreneurship in Macedonia

Veland Ramadani, Gadaf Rexhepi, Léo-Paul Dana, Shqipe Gërguri-Rashiti, and Vanessa Ratten

Abstract This chapter provides a resourceful information about the development of entrepreneurship and small and medium-sized enterprises in the Republic of Macedonia. Mainly, the current state of entrepreneurship, business environment, and problems of entrepreneurs and small business owners are discussed. The chapter ends with suggestions for further development of entrepreneurship in the future.

1 Introduction

This chapter is about entrepreneurship and small and medium-sized companies in the Republic of Macedonia—one of the successor states of former Yugoslavia. It is a small country, located on the Central Balkan Peninsula, in South-Eastern Europe. The Republic of Macedonia declared its independence on September 8, 1991. The country became member of United Nations under the provisional reference of the Former Yugoslav Republic of Macedonia, abbreviated as FYROM, due to the name issue dispute with Greece (United Nations 1993). It covers 25,713 km^2 (9928 square miles), bordering Albania (west), Bulgaria (east), Greece (south), and Kosovo and Serbia (north). Skopje, the capital and the city of Mother Teresa, is the largest city of the country and inhabited by 30% of the total population. The Republic of Macedonia

V. Ramadani (✉) · G. Rexhepi
South-East European University, Tetovo, Macedonia
e-mail: v.ramadani@seeu.edu.mk; g.rexhepi@seeu.edu.mk

L.-P. Dana
Montpellier Business School, Montpellier, France
e-mail: lp.dana@montpellier-bs.com

S. Gërguri-Rashiti
American College of the Middle-East, Eqaila, Kuwait
e-mail: shqipe.gerguri-rashiti@acm.edu.kw

V. Ratten
La Trobe University, Melbourne, Australia
e-mail: v.ratten@latrobe.edu.au

© Springer International Publishing AG, part of Springer Nature 2018   67
R. Palalić et al. (eds.), *Entrepreneurship in Former Yugoslavia*,
https://doi.org/10.1007/978-3-319-77634-7_5

Exhibit 1 Skopje's Old Bazaar. Photo © Veland Ramadani

is a landlocked country, but enriched with many gorgeous mountains, valleys, lakes, and rivers. Most of the tourists would have seen the Macedonian landmarks, such as Sharr Mountains, Ohrid Lake, or for sure they have tasted the delicious coffee on the edge of the Vardar River. The Skopje's Old Bazaar (Exhibit 1), since at least the twelfth century, with its landmarks (Kale Fortress, Bezisten, Stone Bridge, Çifte Hamam, Clock tower, Daut Pasha Hamam, Kurşumli Han, Mustafa Pasha Mosque, and Church of the Holy Salvation), recently became a real touristic attraction.

Based on State Statistical Office of the Republic of Macedonia (2016a, b), in this country live 2,072,490 inhabitants, which is 2.46% more comparing with the census taken in 2002, and 79.7% more comparing with the census of 1948. Based on the Census of 2002, the population of the Republic of Macedonia, with respect to ethnicity, consists of 1,297,981 Macedonians (64.2%); 509,083 Albanians (25.2%); 77,959 Turks (3.9%); 53,879 Romani (2.7%); 35,939 Serbs (1.8%); 19,571 Bosnians/Muslims (0.9%); and 30,688 under the heading of "others" (1.4%).

2 Historical Overview[1]

Although the Ottoman Empire lost Serbia as well as Montenegro in 1878, the sultan kept his hold on Macedonia, a region that had been Turkish since 1371. Unlike Slovenia, Croatia, and Bosnia & Herzegovina, which had been governed by the Austro-Hungarian Empire, Macedonia did not experience Occidental rule, until the

---

[1]This section is based on Dana (1998, 2010).

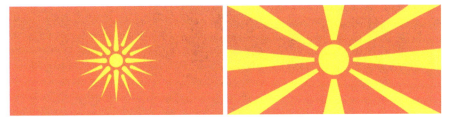

Exhibit 2 The old (Vergina Sun) and the actual flag of the Republic of Macedonia

Balkan Wars (1912–1913), when Macedonia was partitioned into three. Aegean Macedonia would be henceforth governed by Greece; Pirin Macedonia by Bulgaria; and Vardar Macedonia would join the Kingdom of Serbs, Croats, and Slovenes (Yugoslavia as of 1929). Although the monarchy officially joined the Axis in 1941, much of the population resisted such an alliance. In response to this resistance, the Nazis occupied most of Yugoslavia, until 1943.

As it was noted, the Republic of Macedonia declared its independence on September 8, 1991, and obtained international recognition on December 19 that same year. On February 6, 1992, Turkey recognized the independence of the Republic of Macedonia. Greece strongly opposed recognition of Macedonia's independence, claiming that the whole area should be a Greek province. Furthermore, Greece was angered by the use of the name Macedonia, which also refers to a region in northern Greece. As well, Greece protested that the new republic should not be allowed to include the 16-point sun on its flag (Vergina Sun symbol; Exhibit 2), as this symbol is Greek in origin. The reaction of Greece, in 1992, was to impose an embargo on Macedonia and the Macedonian economy slowed down. Nevertheless, the Macedonians continued to have access to a wide variety of Greek products, as smuggling by entrepreneurs helped many items find their way into Macedonian shops. Empty Pepsi cans and wrappers from "Kiss" brand chocolate bars, both from Greece, littered the streets of Skopje, the Macedonian capital. Finally, in September 1995, the United States brokered an end to the embargo when Macedonia accepted to change its flag (Exhibit 2) as well as its name, such as to exclude possible symbolism for territorial expansion.

Once the Republic of Macedonia agreed to change its name to FYROM—the acronym for the Former Yugoslav Republic of Macedonia—the embargo was lifted. This change of name legalized international trade, thereby increasing opportunities for entrepreneurship. Those who exhibit entrepreneurial behavior are often Macedonians who have worked abroad. Meanwhile, at home in the Republic of Macedonia, once-subsidized prices have skyrocketed, as has unemployment; the elderly have suffered the most (Exhibit 3).

Especially among retired people who cannot compete in the new system, there is still nostalgia for the good old days of unity under Tito, whose portrait is admired across the country. His name comes up often in discussions (Exhibit 4).

Exhibit 3 No longer employed. Photo © Léo-Paul Dana

Exhibit 4 Nostalgic for Tito. Photo © Léo-Paul Dana

Today, the Republic of Macedonia is a member of the United Nations and the Council of Europe. In 2005, this country became a candidate for joining the European Union (EU) and in 2008 applied (Bucharest Summit) to join the North

Exhibit 5 Square "Macedonia" in Skopje. Photo © Veland Ramadani

Atlantic Treaty Organization (NATO), but unfortunately, the accession in these structures remained "captivated" by the name dispute with Greece. During the period when a solution might have been possible, the Government of the Republic of Macedonia, led by Nikola Gruevski, launched one of the most controversial and meaningless "Skopje 2014" project, which involved building the Statue of Alexander the Great on the Skopje's main square "Macedonia" (Exhibit 5) and setting up several statues of mainly ethnic Macedonian's historical figures; these activities were considered by Greece as a direct provocation, and all this increased more and more frustrations on the name issue and exacerbated the relations with the Republic of Macedonia. This created also a reaction to the Ethnic Albanians, who built their "own" square on the "other side of Vardar River" and named it "Scanderbeg Square" (Exhibit 6).

The new Government of the Republic of Macedonia, led by Zoran Zaev, established in May 2017, initiated numerous bilateral and multilateral meetings with the Greek Government and international organizations, in order to find an adequate solution of this issue, which will not hurt the "nationalist" feelings of both countries and nations. There is a hope!

3 Environment for Entrepreneurship

3.1 Current State of Entrepreneurship and SMEs

The broad economic literature confirms that entrepreneurship and small and medium-sized enterprises (SMEs) represent the backbone of all economies. They represent a vital segment of the economic structure of each country. The role of

Exhibit 6 Square "Scanderbeg" in Skopje. Photo © Veland Ramadani

Table 1 EU enterprise classification criteria

Enterprise category	No. of employees	Turnover (€)	Balance sheet (€)
Micro	<10	≤2 million	≤2 million
Small	<50	≤10 million	≤10 million
Medium	<250	≤50 million	≤43 million

Source: European Commission (2005, p. 14)

entrepreneurship and small and medium-sized enterprises is reflected in the possibility of opening new jobs, using resources at the local level, introducing innovations, increasing competition, and thus the quality of products and services, thus
contributing to a better life of the population (Hisrich and Ramadani 2017).

Following the adoption of the European Charter for Small Enterprises in June
2000 by the European Council, there was a need for a better definition and regulation
of microenterprises. As a result, the European Commission has introduced this new
category of enterprises (European Commission 2005) among other changes. The
criteria used by the European Union to determine the type of enterprises are: number
of employees, turnover, and balance sheet. The new European Union (EU) definition,
which is applicable from 1 January 2005, according to the above-mentioned criteria,
divides the enterprises as indicated in Table 1.

In the Republic of Macedonia, small and medium-sized enterprises are defined
according to the Law on Trade Companies, in which the above-mentioned EU criteria
for classification of enterprises were accepted and incorporated, normally adapted to
the country's economic conditions. The Law on Trade Companies introduced the
term micro-trader for the first time. Therefore, according to the provisions of the Law
(Article 470), enterprises are classified as micro, small, medium, and large

Table 2 Classification of enterprises in the Republic of Macedonia

Enterprise category	No. of employees	Turnover (€)	Balance sheet
Micro	<10	≤50,000	–
Small	<50	≤2 million	≤2 million
Medium	<250	≤10 million	≤11 million

Table 3 Active enterprises in the Republic of Macedonia for the period 2010–2015

Year	Total	Micro	Small	Medium	Large
2015	70,139	63,590	4979	1339	231
2014	70,659	64,187	4961	1305	206
2013	71,290	65,014	4776	1291	209
2012	74,424	68,211	4732	1280	201
2011	73,118	67,294	4452	1187	185
2010	75,497	70,032	4051	1211	203

enterprises, i.e., traders (Official Gazette of the Republic of Macedonia 2004), as indicated in Table 2.

According to the data of the State Statistical Office of the Republic of Macedonia (2016a, b), in 2015, 70,139 enterprises were active in the Republic of Macedonia. Among them, 63,590 were microenterprises, 4979 small, 1339 medium, and 231 large enterprises (Table 3). Enterprises with 0–9 employees have the largest share of 90.66%. in the total number of enterprises. Then come enterprises with 10–50 employees, who participate with 7.10%, 50–250 employees with 1.91%, and finally enterprises with over 250 employees participate with 0.33%. According to the sectoral distribution, the major sectors are: Wholesale and retail; repair of motor vehicles and motorcycles with 23,843 enterprises (34.0%), and processing industry with 7639 enterprises (10.9%), while the smallest share are mining and quarrying with 173 enterprises (0.2%) and supply with electricity, gas, steam, and air conditioning with 160 enterprises (0.2%).

The Global Entrepreneurship Monitor (GEM) provides a valuable and irreplaceable base of information about entrepreneurs across different countries. The entrepreneurial activity of a particular country is measured through the Total Early-Stage Entrepreneurial Activity (TEA) index—the percentage of people aged 18–64 who are in the process of starting a new business or already are running a new business (not older than 42 months). The TEA index involves two groups of individuals:

- Individuals who enter into business by establishing their own business due to *necessity (necessity-driven entrepreneurs)*, respectively, because they weren't able to find a better employment opportunity.
- Individuals who enter into business because of perceiving an *opportunity (opportunity-driven entrepreneurs)*, through which they will achieve greater income and greater independence.

The TEA index in the Republic of Macedonia is showing a decreasing tendency (GEM Macedonia 2014). Namely, the TEA index in 2008 was 14.5%, in 2010 it fell to 7.9%, continuing to decline in 2012 and 2013 to 6.97%, i.e., 6.63%. If these indicators would be compared with countries in the region and with the average of the countries in the European Union (8%), the TEA Index of the Republic of Macedonia is the lowest, with exception of Slovenia (which belongs to the innovation-driven group of countries, while the Republic of Macedonia belongs to the efficiency-driven group of countries). Bosnia and Herzegovina has the highest TEA index of 10.34%. Croatia has a TEA index of 8.27%, where the entrepreneurship in the early stage is 6.33% and is related to Croatia's entry into the European Union, thus opening new market opportunities for Croatian entrepreneurs. In addition, in the Republic of Macedonia, in 2013, 60.98% of entrepreneurs stated that they established their own businesses based on necessity and only 22.95% based on perceived opportunity. This indicator (based on necessity) is the highest, if compared with countries in the region and the average of the European Union, which is only 22.70% (Table 4).

In terms of employment (Table 5), in SMEs 264,839 persons are employed, i.e., 74.96% of the total number of employees in the active enterprises in the country. Individually, 116,231 (32.90%) persons are employed in micro, 78,740 (22.29%) in small, 69,868 (19.78%) in medium, and 88,473 (25.04%) in large enterprises. In addition, SMEs participate with 54.1% in the Gross Domestic Product (GDP) of the Republic of Macedonia.

Women entrepreneurship data in certain countries and region can also be found in GEM reports (Ratten et al. 2017). As stated by Sarfaraz and Faghih (2011, p. 52), "GEM's contribution to providing consistent cross-country information and measurement of women's entrepreneurial activity are useful tools to identify entrepreneurial dimensions and rank different countries in this field as well." Moreover, Hontz and Rotanu (2010, p. 8) note that lack of official information about women entrepreneurs represents an important obstacle to trustworthy research, since a "base set of measures cannot be shown to decision-makers." Based on the data published in the GEM Reports, according to TEA index for women, women from Montenegro, Croatia, Serbia, Bosnia and Herzegovina, and Greece are active in efforts to establish/manage any personal business. As it is shown below (Exhibit 7), the TEA index for the Republic of Macedonia, Romania, Slovenia, and Turkey is around 3% (Allen et al. 2008; Kelley et al. 2011; Palalić et al. 2017).

The number of women entrepreneurs in the Republic of Macedonia which is around 18% (Exhibit 8) is higher compared to Albania; however, in comparison to other countries in regions such as Slovenia, Croatia, Bosnia and Herzegovina, Serbia, Romania, and Bulgaria is lower (Sabarwal and Terrell 2008).

The Association of Women Organizations in Macedonia is one of the few initiatives in the Republic of Macedonia that make some efforts to raise awareness about the role of women in the economy and society in general. On the other hand, a number of NGOs take active policy actions aimed in motivating and engaging women in economic and political life. To increase women's involvement in the economic and political life, governmental support is essential, in spite of their

Table 4 The TEA index for the Republic of Macedonia, countries in the region, and the EU

Country	Nascent business	New businesses	Total early-stage entrepreneurial activity (TEA)	Established businesses	Discontinuation	TEA—based on necessity	TEA—based on opportunity
Macedonia 2008	7.20	7.70	14.50	11.00	5.30	47.17	13.45
Macedonia 2010	4.80	3.10	7.90	7.60	1.60	59.00	23.00
Macedonia 2012	3.73	3.25	6.97	6.73	3.86	51.95	28.73
Macedonia 2013	3.35	3.53	6.63	7.29	3.30	60.98	22.95
Bosnia and Herzegovina	5.75	4.64	10.34	4.51	6.18	58.95	22.04
Croatia	6.33	1.98	8.27	3.28	4.51	37.40	29.84
Slovenia	3.58	2.87	6.45	5.68	2.59	24.06	53.42
European union (EU)	4.80	3.30	8.00	6.40	2.90	22.70	47.00

Note: **Nascent business** is considered the businesses/individuals who have decided to undertake a specific business venture, hired resources for start, and even started with initial business operations and paid salaries for the first 3 months
New business is considered the businesses/individuals who paid salaries in the period after the first 3 months (with which they completed the start-up phase) and up to 3.5 years of starting the business
Established businesses are considered those that function for more than 3.5 years
Discontinuation is the last stage of the business life cycle and involves the discontinuity of the business (either by selling, shutting down, or otherwise discontinuing an owner/management relationship with the business)
Source: GEM Macedonia (2014: 30)

Table 5 Number of employees by enterprise size and industry

Industry	Number of employees by enterprise size					
	Total 0–9		10–19	20–49	50–249	250+
Mining and quarrying	4178	333	285	620	399	2541
Manufacturing industry	108,566	14,305	8018	14,117	35,840	36,286
Electricity, gas, steam, and air conditioning supply	7974	171	100	28	582	7093
Water supply, waste water disposal, waste management, and remediation activities	10,193	532	329	680	3291	5361
Construction	28,022	8506	3759	4708	6057	4992
Wholesale and retail; repair of motor vehicles and motorcycles	92,606	50,176	10,601	10,997	10,865	9967
Transport and storage	30,842	11,849	3596	3934	4001	7462
Accommodation facilities and food service activities	19,821	10,498	3937	3244	1874	268
Information and communications	11,463	2482	1414	1512	2171	3884
Real estate activities	2193	664	306	353	572	298
Professional, scientific, and technical activities	18,651	13,482	2335	1673	1161	
Administrative and support service activities	17,697	2235	786	1300	3055	10,321
Repair of computers and personal and household goods	1106	998	57	51	–	–
Total	353,312	116,231	35,523	43,217	69,868	88,473

Source: State Statistical Office of the Republic of Macedonia (2016a, b)

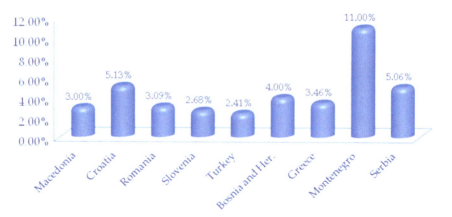

Exhibit 7 Tea index for women entrepreneurs in the Balkan countries. Source: Allen et al. (2008, p. 12), and Kelley et al. (2011, p. 19)

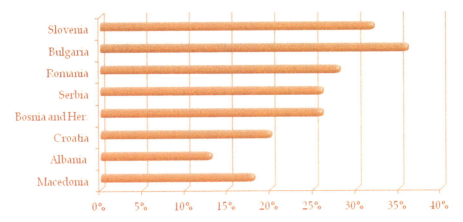

Exhibit 8 Share of women entrepreneurs by country. Source: Based on Sabarwal and Terrell (2008, p. 44)

available human potential and capabilities for successful development of women entrepreneurship. Sadly, the Republic of Macedonia is quite far from adopting these provisions. The founding of the Association of Women Entrepreneurs APNA in June 1999, and NIZA in Skopje, positions women a step forward in this field. The increasing awareness among women to exercise their right to work and afford a better life through support of their ideas reaches higher level day by day. Through the governmental support whether material or immaterial women slowly but surely will find their place and role in the Macedonian economy (Ramadani et al. 2013; Tašaminova 2012).

3.2 Business Environment

Recently, the Republic of Macedonia has marked significant improvements in the general business environment. According to Doing Business 2016 Report, the Republic of Macedonia is ranked 12th out of 189 countries (World Bank 2016). However, in certain segments of the general business environment, immense changes are needed. In some of these segments, things have been improved or are in the process to be improved, and in some of them, a significant slowdown is noted. Regarding the key segments that make up the overall business environment, the situation in this country is as follows:

Property Rights Good protection of property rights, effective execution of contracts, and rule of law in general are mostly related to encouragements and development of entrepreneurial activities. Although in the protection of property rights significant improvements are noted, it still remains a real challenge for the Republic of Macedonia. According to the International Property Rights Index (2015), out of 129 countries analyzed, the Republic of Macedonia is in the 66th position, a position that shows that property rights are not well protected in this country. The property rights index in 2015 includes a total of 10 variables, divided into three main components: legal and political environment, physical property rights, and intellectual property rights. According to the main components of the international index on the legal and political environment chart, the Republic of Macedonia has 4.5 points, which is one percentage point higher than the 2013 index (4.4) and is ranked in the 64th position. Regarding physical property rights, the country has 6.1 points, which is less than in 2013 (6.2), and is ranked as 46th. In the field of intellectual property rights, the Republic of Macedonia is in the 84th place (4.3 points). In comparison with the countries in the region, Republic of Macedonia is ranked better than Serbia (115) and Albania (119), while it is behind the EU Balkan countries, Slovenia (54th place) Croatia (74th), Bulgaria (66th), and Romania (65th), which are ranked 20–30 places higher than the Republic of Macedonia (International Property Rights Index 2015). All this confirms that the judiciary in the Republic of Macedonia does not provide adequate protection of property rights.

Corruption Corruption in the organs of the system, especially in the judiciary and public administration, remains an "incurable wound" in the Republic of Macedonia. According to Transparency International Perception of Corruption Index for 2015, the Republic of Macedonia is ranked 66th out of 167 countries. According to Transparency International (2015) study, on the question "which sectors/institutions are most affected by corruption", the answers were as follow: 68% of respondents responded political parties, 68% judiciary, 55% public administration, 53% police, 53% health, etc., while in the last 12 months, 19% of respondents declared that have corrupted police officers and 16% judges. According to the EBRD (2006), despite the fact that in the Republic of Macedonia (and in transition countries in general) a certain reduction of corruption is noted in all its three main forms of existence: bribe tax (a percentage of total sales of enterprises), kickback tax (a percentage of the value of contracts in the form of additional and unofficial payments to ensure receipt of contracts), and bribery frequency (percentage of respondents who said they accepted to pay bribes in customs, tax administration, etc.), it still remains a relevant problem (Fiti and Ramadani 2013). Thus, state institutions need to take more concrete and rigorous actions in this direction, which will shorten the lengthy court procedures, simplify the complicated procedures for obtaining different permits, facilitate the introduction and transfer of new technologies, consistently protect intellectual property, etc. This may increase the entry rate of high-growth potential small and medium-sized enterprises and the interest of investors.

Administrative–Bureaucratic Obstacles Long administrative–bureaucratic procedures (expressed through the number of necessary procedures and days for starting a new business) are a serious impediment of doing business. Studies show a strong correlation between the administrative-bureaucratic procedures and corruption—the more procedures, the greater the possibility of corruption (Fiti 2008). The Republic of Macedonia has made a significant improvement in this respect. The introduction of the one-stop shop system in 2006 (the law was enacted in September 2005) contributed to a significant reduction of procedures and time for starting a new business. The required time for registration of new enterprises is reduced from 48 to 1 day, while the number of procedures is reduced to only 1. This contributed, based on Doing Business 2016 Report, the Republic of Macedonia to be ranked as a 2nd out of 189 analyzed countries. But, with regard to the closing business issue, this country is ranked as 115th, as this activity takes 1.8 years (World Bank 2016).

Tax Policy In 2007, the Republic of Macedonia introduced the flat tax, which reduced the tax burden on the enterprises. Income tax paid by businesses initially decreased from 15% to 12%, while in the beginning of 2008, it decreased to 10%. The existing three marginal tax rates for personal income tax (15%, 18%, and 24%) were replaced with one rate—10%. In 2016, all contributions that were directly related to salaries of employees were reduced as follows: pension and disability insurance from 19% to 17.5% (this percentage is shared between state and private pension funds), health insurance from 7.5% to 7.3%, and unemployment insurance from 1.4% to 1.2% (Law on Compulsory Social Insurance Contributions 2015).

State Regulation In the area of state regulation, it is necessary to strengthen the autonomy of the regulatory bodies, which would ensure fair and predictable regulation of the market failure domains (public goods, asymmetric information, externalities, existence of monopolies, unequal distribution of income, etc.) as well as deregulation, i.e., removing numerous administrative-bureaucratic obstacles, which hinder the faster development of businesses (Fiti 2008). According to the Global Competitiveness Report 2015/16, the Republic of Macedonia is ranked 60th out of 140 countries, rated with 4.28, where 1 is the worst, while 7 is the best rating (Schwab 2015, p. 7).

Infrastructure Infrastructure, such as roads, railways, airports, telecommunications, energy, etc. has a significant impact on the business costs. The 2015 World Economic Forum Report about the quality of the infrastructure ranked the Republic of Macedonia in 77th place (out of 140 analyzed countries), or individually, for the quality of roads in the 88th place, railways in 85th place, energy 66th place, and telecommunications in the 61st place. Airports are ranked in the best position, where Republic of Macedonia is ranked in 50th place (Schwab 2015, p. 243). Skopje's Airport is shown in Exhibit 9.

The Republic of Macedonia, in order to stimulate the development of entrepreneurship and SMEs, should provide a favorable, friendly business environment which implies good protection of property rights, efficient execution of contracts, rule of law, quality and non-arbitral regulation, stable and predictable government policy, corruption, elimination of administrative–bureaucratic barriers, providing favorable tax policy, moreover providing broad and absorption power on the market, etc.

From January 2008, the Republic of Macedonia officially started the implementation of the European Union Competitiveness and Innovation Programme (CIP) for the period of 2007–2013, which became the second country after Croatia, which is not part of the EU but is part of this program. CIP is particularly important for small and medium enterprise in the Republic of Macedonia, which would support them in

Exhibit 9   Airport "Alexander the Great" in Skopje. Photo © Veland Ramadani

becoming international, have better access to financial resources, better usage of information and communication technologies, and development of the technological society.

Nowadays, there are several ministries, agencies, and organizations that are actively involved to enforce the promotion and formulation of the national entrepreneurship policy, such as (Dana 2010; Ramadani 2013; Rexhepi 2014): Ministry of Economy (MoE), Ministry of Education and Science (MoES), Ministry of Information Society and Administration (MoISA), Agency for promotion of entrepreneurship of the Republic of Macedonia (APPRM), Macedonian Bank for Development Promotion (MBDP), Fund for Innovation and Technology Development, Department for Entrepreneurship and Competitiveness of SMEs, Department for Industrial policy, Department for the Advancement of Science and Technological-Technical Development, Agency for Financial Support in Agriculture and Rural Development (IPARD), Centre for Entrepreneurship and Executive Development (CEED), etc. Besides this, several programs and instruments have been put in place to increase entrepreneurship capacities, such as: Central European Initiative Know-how Exchange Programme (CEI-KEP), Competitiveness and Innovation Framework Programme (CIP), European Fund for the Balkans (EFB), Instrument for Pre-Accession Assistance (IPA), Open Regional Fund for Foreign Trade Promotion in South-East Europe (ORF), Technology Transfer Project, GIZ (German International Cooperation Program), USAID Macedonia (Macedonia Competitiveness Project, Small and Medium Enterprise Development Credit Authority (SME DCA) (2007–2014), USAID Business without Borders Project (2011–2013), Creative Business Project (2010–2013), USAIDs GDA Digital Media Park (2006-open end), and USAID Microenterprise Funding and Learning for Growth Project (2011–2016).

3.3   Problems and Challenges Faced by Entrepreneurs

Many SMEs are extinguished, disappearing every year due to different reasons, for example: the management is not well trained and does not have enough business experience; owners decide by themselves for all issues, which indicate the absence of specialization in certain functions; product and services assortment is not sufficiently diversified; serious financing problems, etc. All these features make them particularly risky businesses (Ramadani 2014).

Entrepreneurs usually face various problems and challenges. Some of them appear before and some after starting the business (Ramadani et al. 2015). According to Shuklev (2015), entrepreneurs in the Republic of Macedonia are facing these problems and challenges commonly: lack of initial capital, complicated legislation, problems with suppliers, lack of professional staff, etc. Ramadani and Gërguri (2011) in his research with a sample of 119 domestic SMEs found these problems and challenges: confronting with unfair competition (29.96% of respondents), payment problems (21.59%), decline in sales (18.94%), lack of qualitative financial assets (12.78%), legal regulation (10.13%), lack of adequate human resources (3.52%), others (3.08%).

As can be seen from these two studies, among the major problems and challenges of entrepreneurs in the Republic of Macedonia are those related to lack of professional staff, lack of qualitative funding sources, inability to deal with legal regulation related to doing business, and lack of business-related experience and knowledge.

4   Toward the Future

4.1   Initiating and Developing Venture Capital as a High-Quality Source of Financing

Experiences from developed countries confirm that many enterprises, such as Ford, Amazon, Microsoft, Bell Telephone, Apple Computers, etc., due to the help of venture capital have risen high in the scale of successful businesses. Therefore, this type of financing small and medium-sized enterprises should be constantly stimulated and a larger number of entities that deal with this issue, or that can make a significant contribution to its development, should be involved (Ramadani 2009). Venture capital, as an important financing source, is almost completely absent in the Republic of Macedonia, which makes Macedonian SMEs deprived of one of the most favorable and highest quality sources for financing their development.

Venture capital is consisted of financial means in the form of equity capital and know-how management, which are invested by individuals and institutions in SMEs, which are not listed on the stock market and have high growth potential (Mason and Botelho 2016; Ramadani 2014).

Principally, venture capital appears in two basic forms: informal venture capital, i.e., business angels and formal venture capital. Business angels, as informal venture capitalists, represent private investors who, through their active work, have gained wealth and experience and are willing to invest in new SMEs in order to help young entrepreneurs, and normally, make a profit for themselves. Business angels are a particularly interesting solution for the new small and medium-sized enterprises, but also for those existing, who have promising and alluring ideas and projects, but face a lack of finance. Their significance is especially great in the early stages of development of enterprises. As patient investors, they direct entrepreneurs on the right path of enterprise management and development and provide venture capital and knowledge. Business angels play an increasingly important role in financing many new businesses, although compared to other sources of financing, individually, they invest relatively small amounts of money (Cumming and Zhang 2016; Mason 2006). Business angels, lately, to increase their significance, establish business angel groups (syndicates) and networks. Business angel groups are business angel associations that merge their capital, experience, and knowledge in order to share risk, make a better evaluation of projects, and invest in better and bigger deals, while business angel networks are organizations whose main goal is linking entrepreneurs and business angels.

Formal venture capital represents the capital mobilized from pension funds, insurance companies, corporations, financial institutions, academic institutions, individuals, etc. by venture capital firm, which manages and invests it in small and medium-sized enterprises that do not quote on the stock exchange, in a limited time period, in order to realize profit for themselves, investors, and entrepreneurs. Venture capital firm together with investors forms a partnership in which the venture capital firm appears as a general partner, while investors appear as limited partners.

Venture capitalists' specialty is that, beside money, they invest time and expertise. The notion of *time and expertise* suggests that venture capitalists have significant entrepreneurial and managerial experiences; knowledge about the sector are important for strategic decisions and solving serious problems and challenges, which enables them to directly be involved in enterprises in which they invest (Fiti and Ramadani 2013). Precisely, because of these benefits, they are known as "smart money."

In the Republic of Macedonia, there is no special law for regulating venture capital, especially business angels (as in the United States, Great Britain, Turkey, etc.). Informally, initiatives have been in place since 2006, but until now such law does not exist in the country. In the Republic of Macedonia, there is a legal framework only for the establishment of venture capital funds. The establishment and operation of these funds can be regulated in accordance with the Law on Investment Funds (since 2000, which has been amended in 2007, 2009, 2013), which enables the establishment of private funds, and the way it functions is very similar to venture capital funds.

4.2 Subsidizing Research and Development Process for Innovative Products and Services for Domestic SMEs and Establishment of Business Incubators and Technology Parks in Universities and Larger Municipalities

Today, in the era of globalization, companies face intense competition. Today's enterprises are under great pressure from other companies that offer the same or similar product or service or under pressure from consumers who expect more and more of the product they consume (Ramadani et al. 2017). The Bureau for Intellectual Property Protection of the Republic of Macedonia, in the 1990s, conducted a survey to find out the reasons for undertaking innovative activities by Macedonian companies. The respondents answered that they undertook innovative activities for the following reasons: improvement of the products' quality (15.67% of the respondents), achieving access to new markets (13.07%), protection of the existing markets (12.77%), decreasing production costs (12.57%), improvement of working methods (9.68%), etc. (Ministry of Economy of the Republic of Macedonia 2004, p. 49).

According to State Statistical Office of the Republic of Macedonia (2014), 39.9% of the small enterprises are innovative, where the most innovative are the enterprises in the field of finance and insurance (89.1%), followed by information and communication enterprises (69.5%), enterprises dealing with real estate (59.5%), while the least innovative are construction, transportation, and agricultural enterprises. But here needs to be emphasized that the majority of innovations are related to organization and marketing, while only 24.7% of innovations refer to new and improved products or processes. In addition, 91.6% of innovators of products or processes act on domestic market and 59.5% of the funds intended for innovation go for supplying equipment, machines, software, and buildings that can, but do not have to lead to development of innovative products and processes. This data shows that entrepreneurs in this country have not yet understood enough the role of innovation for the growth and development of their enterprises.

Entrepreneurs in the Republic of Macedonia need to maximize the number of innovative products and services, which would increase their competitiveness, not only in the domestic but also in the international market (Rexhepi et al. 2017). The Government of the Republic of Macedonia (Exhibit 10) can play a significant role in this process through financial support of the research and development process and by engaging foreign proven experts in the field of innovation. A good start is the establishment of the Fund for Innovation and Technological Development in 2013, but the funds that are provided to support innovation are very symbolic (2000–5000 euros) and do not represent a real support in this difficult, but extremely important process (Dzambazovski 2015, p. 10). According to World Bank data for 2013, in the

Exhibit 10 The Government of the R. of Macedonia. Photo © Veland Ramadani

Republic of Macedonia, the expenditures for research and development account only 0.44% of GDP of the country. In the regional countries, the situation is as follows: Serbia −0.73%, Croatia −0.81%, Bulgaria −0.65%, Slovenia −2.59%, and Montenegro with 0.38%. In addition, beside increase of research and development expenditures, the government can help SMEs through tax credit for the expenditures made for research and development. In this case, the tax credit represents the right to reduce the amount of the corporate income tax (Globerman 2012). Such policies have been successfully applied in United States, Canada, Great Britain, France, etc. The establishment of business incubators and technology parks has proven to be a good measure of increasing innovation in certain countries. It would be desirable for universities in this country, in cooperation with real sector and government help, to create their own business incubators and technology parks in which students would have the opportunity to develop and transform their business ideas into real products and services that would represent solutions to the problems of existing domestic enterprises and, on the other hand, will contribute to the development of new businesses. SEEU TechPark (Exhibit 11), established by South East European University in Tetovo, and Business Start-Up Center, at the University "St. Cyril and Methodius" in Skopje (Faculty of Mechanical Engineering) can be mentioned as success stories.

In addition, the government can set up business incubators and technology parks in larger municipalities and this will contribute to the development of entrepreneurship and SMEs' development, which will be reflected with new jobs creation and increasing the state and municipalities budgets by collecting taxes, contributions, and various fees from newly created businesses.

Exhibit 11 SEEU TechPark. Photo © Veland Ramadani

5   Case Study: Zito Centar DOO[2]

Zito Centar DOO is a Macedonian bakery products manufacturer, founded in 1995. It is one of the leaders in this field, equipped with new machines and well-trained workforce. In the beginning, it used to produce just a few products, namely 1.000 units of bread per day or 30.000 units of bread per month. The production and selling were organized by five workers and two distributors. The factory continued to develop very quickly and surely. Today, Zito Centar DOO has 125 workers and 40 distributors that distribute an amount of 35,000 products per day or 1,050,000 products monthly.

The factory produces a variety of 30 different types of bread. However, among all products, they highlight "Tonus," a bread without flour, made directly from an integral grain, which has been led up to a stage of germination (Exhibit 12). This bread is produced with the purpose of maximal use of all nutrients of the wheat grain. Zito Centar DOO produces it based on the franchise agreement with Russian scientist, Vladimir Antonov.

"Tonus" bread contains plenty of food fibers. A consumption of 250 g of "Tonus" bread per day provides our body with 40–45 g of fibers. A daily norm of 50 g is recommended. According to the data of National Center of Hygiene of Ministry of Health in Bulgaria, the content of alimentary fibers in the "Tonus" bread is 22%. In its volume, it contains 13% soluble food fibers and 9% non-soluble food fibers (FF), which is 20 times more than the amounts found in widespread bread. The enormous value of "Tonus" bread is in the fact that all of the most valuable nutrients in grain

---

[2]This case is written by Orhan Musliu (the company's owner) and Veland Ramadani.

Exhibit 12 The "Tonus" bread. Photo © Zito Centar DOO

come to life at swelling and are prepared for germination, leading to the creation of a new life, the life of sprout. In this type of bread, all morphological parts of a grain including a germ, an aileron layer, and multilayered shells are kept in their biologically active state. These components, including almost all mineral elements and vitamins, are necessary for the organism of an individual.

"Tonus" is very rich in magnesium, zinc, selenium, iron, manganese, copper, cobalt, and silicon. "Tonus" is vitamin-rich: B1, B2, B3 (RR), B6, B12, a folic acid, vitamin E. It has been clinically tested that regular consumption of "Tonus" bread normalizes metabolism; cleanses the body from toxins, carcinogens, and other toxic substances; stabilizes and reduces blood sugar for diabetes patients; cleanses the body from excessive amounts of cholesterol; improves intestinal motor function; reduces overweight; increases hemoglobin in the blood; improves the function of blood renewal; and prevents cancer.

References

Allen, E. I., Elam, A., Langowitz, N., & Dean, M. (2008). *2007 Report on women entrepreneurship*. Babson Park, MA: Babson College.

Cumming, D., & Zhang, M. (2016). *Angel investors around the world*. Retrieved May 15, 2016, from http://ssrn.com/abstract=2716312 or https://doi.org/10.2139/ssrn.2716312

Dana, L.-P. (1998). Waiting for direction in the former Yugoslav Republic of Macedonia (FYROM). *Journal of Small Business Management, 36*(2), 62–67.

Dana, L.-P. (2010). *When economies change hands: A survey of entrepreneurship in the emerging markets of Europe from the Balkans to the Baltic states*. New York: Routledge.

Dzambazovski, N. (2015). *How to support small and medium enterprises (SMEs) in order to become a driver of the Macedonian economy*. Skopje: Progres.

EBRD. (2006). *Transition report: finance in transition*. London: European Bank for Reconstruction and Development.

European Commission. (2005). *The new SME definition: User guide and model declaration*. Brussels: Enterprise and Industry Publications.

Fiti, T. (2008). *Economics*. Skopje: Faculty of Economics.

Fiti, T., & Ramadani, V. (2013). Venture capital initiatives in Macedonia: Current situation, barriers and perspectives (in English). In V. Ramadani & R. C. Schneider (Eds.), *Entrepreneurship in the Balkans: Diversity, support and prospects* (pp. 317–338). Heidelberg: Springer.

GEM Macedonia. (2014). *Entrepreneurship in Macedonia*. Skopje: Macedonian Enterprise Development Foundation.

Globerman, S. (2012). *Public policies to encourage innovation and productivity*. Ottawa: Macdonald-Laurier Institute.

Hisrich, D. R., & Ramadani, V. (2017). *Effective entrepreneurial management*. Cham: Springer.

Hontz, E., & Rotanu, C. (2010). *Women's business associations from around the world: Central and Eastern Europe*. Washington, DC: Center for International Private Enterprise.

International Property Rights Index. (2015). *Macedonia*. Retrieved May 15, 2016, from http://internationalpropertyrightsindex.org/country?c=MACEDONIA

Kelley, J. D., Brush, D. G., Greene, G. P., & Litovsky, Y. (2011). *2010 Report: Women entrepreneurs worldwide*. Babson Park, MA: Babson College.

Law on Compulsory Social Insurance Contributions. (2015). *Article 25 published in the official gazette of the republic of Macedonia*. Skopje: Government of the Republic of Macedonia.

Mason, C. M. (2006). The informal venture capital market in the United Kingdom: Adding the time dimension. In J. E. Butler, A. Lockett, & D. Ucbasaran (Eds.), *Venture capital and the changing world of entrepreneurship*, *Research in entrepreneurship and management* (pp. 137–171). Greenwich: Information Age Publishing.

Mason, C., & Botelho, T. (2016). The role of the exit in the initial screening of investment opportunities: The case of business angel syndicate gatekeepers. *International Small Business Journal, 34*(2), 157–175. Retrieved May 15, 2016, from http://www.gla.ac.uk/media/media_302905_en.pdf

Ministry of Economy of the Republic of Macedonia. (2004). *Observatory for SMEs in the Republic of Macedonia*. Skopje: Government of the Republic of Macedonia.

Official Gazette of the Republic of Macedonia. (2004). *Law on trade companies*. Skopje: Government of the Republic of Macedonia.

Palalić, R., Ramadani, V., & Dana, L.-P. (2017). Entrepreneurship in Bosnia and Herzegovina: Focus on gender. *European Business Review, 29*(4), 476–496.

Ramadani, V. (2009). Business angels: Who they really are. *Strategic Change, 18*(7–8), 249–258.

Ramadani, V. (2013). Entrepreneurship and small business in the republic of Macedonia. *Strategic Change, 22*(7–8), 485–501.

Ramadani, V. (2014). Venture capital financing in the republic of Macedonia: What is done and what should be done? *Journal of Finance and Risk Perspectives, 3*(2), 27–46.

Ramadani, V., & Gërguri, S. (2011). Innovations: principles and strategies. *Strategic Change, 20*(3–4), 101–110.

Ramadani, V., Gërguri, S., Dana, L.-P., & Tašaminova, T. (2013). Women entrepreneurs in the republic of Macedonia: Waiting for directions. *International Journal of Entrepreneurship and Small Business, 19*(1), 95–121.

Ramadani, V., Hisrich, R. D., & Gerguri-Rashiti, S. (2015). Female entrepreneurs in transition economies: Insights from Albania, Macedonia and Kosovo. *World Review of Entrepreneurship, Management and Sustainable Development, 11*(4), 391–413.

Ramadani, V., Abazi-Alili, H., Dana, L.-P., Rexhepi, G., & Ibraimi, S. (2017). The impact of knowledge spillovers and innovation on firm-performance: Findings from the Balkans countries. *International Entrepreneurship and Management Journal, 13*(1), 299–325.

Ratten, V., Ferreira, J., & Fernandes, C. (2017). Balkans entrepreneurship: The role of internal and external knowledge for business creation. *World Review of Entrepreneurship, Management and Sustainable Development, 13*(2–3), 126–140.

Rexhepi, G. (2014). Use the right strategy and grow. *ACRN Journal of Entrepreneurship Perspectives, 3*(1), 19–29.

Rexhepi, G., Ramadani, V., Rahdari, A., & Anggadwita, G. (2017). Models and strategies of family businesses internationalization: A conceptual framework and future research directions. *Review of International Business and Strategy, 27*(2), 248–260.

Sabarwal, S., & Terrell, K. (2008). *Does gender matter for firm performance? Evidence from Eastern Europe and Central Asia.* Washington, DC: World Bank.

Sarfaraz, L., & Faghih, N. (2011). Women's entrepreneurship in Iran: A GEM based-data evidence. *Journal of Global Entrepreneurship Research, 1*(1), 45–57.

Schwab, K. (2015). *Global competitiveness report 2015/16.* Geneva: World Economic Forum.

Shuklev, B. (2015). *Management of small business* (6th ed.). Skopje: Faculty of Economics.

State Statistical Office of the Republic of Macedonia. (2014). *Statistical yearbook of the republic of Macedonia.* Skopje: Government of Republic of Macedonia.

State Statistical Office of the Republic of Macedonia. (2016a). *Macedonia in figures.* Skopje: Government of Republic of Macedonia.

State Statistical Office of the Republic of Macedonia. (2016b, March 07). *Structural business statistics,* press release 6.1.16.17. Skopje: Government of Republic of Macedonia.

Tašaminova, T. (2012). *Women entrepreneurs in Macedonia: Situation, problems and perspectives.* Master thesis, Tetovo, Republic of Macedonia: South-East European University.

Transparency International. (2015). *The 2015 global corruption barometer report.* Retrieved May 10, 2016, from http://www.transparency.org/research/gcb/gcb_2015_16/0/

United Nations. (1993). *Admission of the State whose application is contained in document A/47/876-S/25147 to membership in the United Nations [online].* Retrieved November 22, 2012, from http://www.un.org/documents/ga/res/47/a47r225.htm

World Bank. (2016). *Doing business report 2016.* Washington: The International Bank for Reconstruction and Development/The World Bank.

Veland Ramadani is an associate professor at South-East European University, Republic of Macedonia, where he teaches both undergraduate and postgraduate courses in entrepreneurship and small business management. His research interests include entrepreneurship, small business management, and venture capital investments. He authored or coauthored around 80 research articles and 17 books. Dr. Ramadani is an associate editor of *International Journal of Entrepreneurship and Small Business (IJESB).* Dr. Ramadani received the Award for Excellence 2015—Outstanding Reviewer by Emerald Group Publishing (*Journal of Enterprising Communities: People and Places in the Global Economy*).

Gadaf Rexhepi is associate professor at South-East European University, Republic of Macedonia. He authored more than 40 research papers in different peer and refereed journals around the world. He is also author and coauthor of several text books and monographs, such as: Strategic Management, Total Quality Management, Introduction to Business, Direct Marketing and Small Business, etc. The author works as a consultant in Business Development Centre at South East European University and is active as an expert in several committees in Ministry of Economy in Macedonia. He actively delivers public lectures in different schools and organizations related to economic and business issues.

Léo-Paul Dana earned BA and MBA degrees at McGill University and a PhD from HEC-Montreal. He is professor of Entrepreneurship at Montpellier Business School and a member of the Entrepreneurship & Innovation chair of LabEx Entrepreneurship (University of Montpellier, France). He formerly served as visiting professor of Entrepreneurship at INSEAD and deputy director of the International Business MBA Program at Nanyang Business School. He has published extensively in a variety of leading journals including the *British Food Journal, Cornell Quarterly, Entrepreneurship and Regional Development, Entrepreneurship: Theory and Practice, Journal of Small Business Management, Journal of World Business,* and *Small Business Economics.* His research interests focus on cultural issues, including the internationalization of entrepreneurship.

Shqipe Gërguri-Rashiti is the dean of Business College at American College of the Middle East (Kuwait). She teaches mostly undergraduate courses in strategic management. Her research interests include management, strategic management, management information systems, etc. She authored around twenty research articles. Besides being a lecturer, she has been also involved in managing different UNDP projects. In January 2016, Dr. Gërguri-Rashiti was awarded for Outstanding Teaching and Learning by American University of the Middle-East, Kuwait. Among her recent books is the *Female Entrepreneurship in Transition Economies.*

Vanessa Ratten is an associate professor (Entrepreneurship and Innovation) at La Trobe Business School, La Trobe University. She is the discipline coordinator of Entrepreneurship and Innovation at La Trobe Business School. She teaches undergraduate, postgraduate, and executive education courses on entrepreneurship, innovation, sport innovation, management, and marketing for sustainable value creation and entrepreneurial business planning. Her main research areas include entrepreneurship (especially sport entrepreneurship, developing country entrepreneurship and international entrepreneurship) and innovation (focusing on technological innovation, cloud computing, mobile commerce).

Entrepreneurship in Montenegro

Ramo Palalić, Azra Bičo, Veland Ramadani, and Léo-Paul Dana

Abstract In this chapter, the entrepreneurial activities and actual policies for the development of entrepreneurship in Montenegro are described. The study begins with providing a historical overview of Montenegro since its establishment, starting from its early times, throughout the Ottoman Empire and up to these days, when Montenegro is also one of the candidates from ex-Yugoslavia's republics to join the EU and NATO (already a member). Then, the study further discusses the promotional activities of entrepreneurship and the role of the government in creating a favorable environment for domestic and foreign entrepreneurs. The chapter ends with providing useful future development of entrepreneurship in Montenegro. It includes, beside tables and figures, original pictures of the business environment in Montenegro.

1 Introduction

Like other ex-Yugoslavian republics, Montenegro is today an independent state. It is located in the west-central Balkan, and it is in the southern part of the former Yugoslavia. Montenegro borders with Bosnia and Herzegovina (north-west), Croatia (west-coastal line), Serbia (north-east), Kosovo (east), and Albania (south-east). The total area of Montenegro is 13,812 km^2. The estimated population of Montenegro in 2016 is 623,000 (Statistical Office of Montenegro—MONSTAT 2017). The capital city is Podgorica with its population of 173,000. Border length is 614 km, and coastal side length is 293 km (Exhibit 1).

R. Palalić (✉) · A. Bičo
International University of Sarajevo, Sarajevo, Bosnia and Herzegovina
e-mail: rpalalic@ius.edu.ba

V. Ramadani
South-East European University, Tetovo, Macedonia

L.-P. Dana
Montpellier Business School, Montpellier, France

© Springer International Publishing AG, part of Springer Nature 2018
R. Palalić et al. (eds.), *Entrepreneurship in Former Yugoslavia*,
https://doi.org/10.1007/978-3-319-77634-7_6

Temelji se na zemljovidu Kartografskoga odsjeka Ujedinjenih Naroda broj (No.) 4274 iz srpnja 2006.

Exhibit 1 Map of Montenegro. Source: Montenegro, Map No. 4274, July 2006, UNITED NATIONS. Available on http://www.un.org/Depts/Cartographic/map/profile/montenegro.pdf. Accessed on December 19, 2017

The population of Montenegro is very diverse like in neighboring countries. Ethnic groups that exist in the Montenegro land are Montenegrins (43%), Serbians (32%), Bosniaks (12%), Albanians (5%), and other minorities (8%). Accordingly, the official languages used in Montenegro are Montenegrin, Serbian, Bosnian, Albanian, and Croatian.

The terrain of the country is hilly with small valleys in between. The country is famous for beautiful sea and beaches, which places Montenegro as one of the best tourist places in the Adriatic Sea region. The area is rich with old historical architecture like houses and churches as well as modern architecture styles (Exhibits 2 and 3).

Montenegro is a *small economic system*, which has potentials in some industrial sectors like tourism and agriculture. A fair neighbor play in the last years made the country more open to other economies from which it will gain in the long term.

The history, a state of entrepreneurship, and its future will be discussed in the following sections.

Exhibit 2 Old downtown of Podgorica, the capital city. Photo © Ramo Palalić

Exhibit 3 The palace of 'King Nikola'. Source: Governement of Montenegro (2017)

2 Historical Overview

The name Montenegro (Black Mountain) comes from the black mountain, very famous in Montenegro, "Lovcen (Exhibit 4) (in local tongue Lovćen)." This mountain is one of the highest (1749 m) in the country and now represents a beautiful national park in Montenegro. It is also much known in Montenegrin poetry, from which anthem of Montenegro was derived. This mountain is known as a mausoleum of Petar II Petrović Njegoš (1813–1851), the king of Montenegro.

Montenegro has a broad history going even back in early second century BC. Some historians claim that Montenegro had been in the sixth century under the different name than now. Ancestors of Montenegrins are called Docleans (in the seventh century) and later on Zetans. The first state was established in the ninth century. The state had many controversies about king's legacy and who will rule the Montenegro. These

Exhibit 4 Lovćen Mountain, Montenegro. Source: Fact Sheet Montenegro (2010)

disagreements were a great opportunity for the Serbian King Dušana (Stefan Dušan Nemanjić, 1308–1355) to occupy Montenegro. Prior the Ottoman Empire in fourteenth centuries, Montenegro had several rebellions under the Serbian ruling.

In 1496, Montenegro lost its formal independence and falls under the Ottoman Empire, but during the sixteenth century, it had established a form of a unique autonomy within the Ottoman Empire. Later, after securing independence from the Ottomans, the Assembly of the Montenegrins appointed Danilo Petrovic as Prince-Bishop (Vladika), Orthodox Metropolitan and ruler, founder of the Petrovic Dynasty (1697–1918) and theocracy in Montenegro (Montenegro Fact Sheet 2010).

In the period from 1784–1830, Vladika Petar I Petrovic had united the people in most of the today's Montenegro and had set the legal foundations of the modern Montenegrin state. Moreover, he had repelled Ottoman attacks and had become one of the most critical men in Montenegro's history. During 1830 and up to 1851, Vladika Petar II Petrovic (Njegos) had ruled the Montenegro, and he had created a stable state apparatus (Montenegro Fact Sheet 2010).

In 1851, Prince Danilo had become the first secular Petrovic ruler, and he had enforced the state centralization. In 1878, on the Congress in Berlin, Montenegro had received full international recognition of independence and sovereignty under the Prince Nikola Petrovic, and in 1910, the Kingdom of Montenegro had been proclaimed under King Nikola I, after adopting the Constitution in 1905 (Montenegro Fact Sheet 2010).

From 1914 to 1916, Montenegro had taken part in World War I on the side of the Allies and won a crucial victory against the much stronger Austria-Hungary. After the assembly in Podgorica in 1918, Montenegro had lost its independence and had joined the Kingdom of Serbs, Croats, and Slovenes (later the Kingdom of Yugoslavia). In the beginning of the World War II (1941), after the capitulation of Yugoslavia, Montenegrins has organized rebellions against German Nazi, and in 1945 Montenegro becomes an equal member of the six-Republic Federation of Yugoslavia (SFRY). After the dissolution of Yugoslavia in 1990, Montenegro formed the Federal Republic of Yugoslavia with Serbia (later the State Union of Serbia and Montenegro), while in 2006, after a referendum on independence on May 21, Montenegro has retrieved independence from the last form of Yugoslavia (Montenegro Fact Sheet 2010). On June 5th, 2017, Montenegro became a 29th NATO member.

3   Environment for Entrepreneurship[1]

Beginning of the entrepreneurship development in Montenegro has started with a change of Regulation of new ventures registration by the Enterprise Law in 2002 across ex-federal Republic Yugoslavia (Serbia and Montenegro state). At the same

---

[1]This section is based on Ramadani V., and Dana, L-P. (2013) in Ramadani and Schneider (Eds. 2013), Entrepreneurship in the Balkans: Diversity, Support and Prospects, Springer.

time, Montenegro commenced a "mass privatization scheme," in which vouchers have been distributed across the country. In 2003, the Act of Modifications of and Supplements to the Act of Privatization of the Economy assured every Montenegrin above 18 years old to have two vouchers. This move has hastened the privatization process and entrepreneurship development. So, in 2003, half of state ownership of Montenegro was privatized, and more than 90% of companies were or to be privatized. In the same year, more than half of Montenegro's population had privatization funds or shares.

The first public support for entrepreneurship development in Montenegro was the establishment of the Center for Entrepreneurship and Economic Development. It was the critical source of consulting and supporting small and medium enterprises (SMEs), new start-ups, or existing organizations.

Moreover, the establishment of the Montenegro Business Alliance (MBA), an association of domestic and foreign business and entrepreneurs, had an impact on business networking internationally and locally. It was primarily related to business to business (B2B) services. Additionally, one of the focuses of the alliance was to retrieve old business links across ex-Yugoslavia.

On the global scale, among 190 countries, doing business for Montenegro is among the last ex-Yugoslavian republics. For instance, Macedonia (10th position) is the best, then Slovenia (30th), Croatia (43rd) Serbia (47th), and then *Montenegro (51st)*. Kosovo is on 60th place and Bosnia and Herzegovina on 81st (Doing Business 2017). This shows that Montenegro has to amend or accept many new Regulations for entrepreneurship development to easily restrict new ventures.

As Montenegro steps forward to the European Union (EU), it is evident that entrepreneurship development improves, like women entrepreneurship as well as social entrepreneurship. Family businesses are also taking place in the socioeconomic development of the country. Being in the "EU castle is a premium (anonymous business owner)" so Montenegrins will be happy to live in and exploit all SMEs advantages that have now EU's ones.

3.1   Economic and Business Environment in Last Two Years[2]

Montenegro, as a small and open economy, has been exposed to outbreaks in 2016 markets that had a reflection on developments in the domestic market. Compared to the previous year, the Montenegrin economy in 2016, according to estimates of the MONSTAT, has achieved positive economic growth rates of 2.5%. During this period, there was a decline in specific indicators such as the fall in total industrial production and total forest production, while in the tourism sector, modest growth rates were recorded about the previous one year, which is partly the result of a high

---

[2]This section is based on the Centralna Banka Crne Gore (2016) (Central Bank of Montenegro).

base from the previous year. A significant growth in the construction sector was recorded, while growth was also recorded in the trade and transport sector.

The annual inflation rate, measured by the consumer price index, in December 2016 amounted to is 1%, while the average annual inflation rate in 2016 was -0.3%. Montenegrin banking system is stable and liquid. However, it is still burdened with low-quality loans, although their level is significantly reduced.

In the year 2016, industrial production declined by 4.4% compared to 2015. Fall of production was recorded in the mining and quarrying sector of 18.1%, and the manufacturing sector from 7.8%, while in the electricity sector, gas and steam supplies were recorded growth of 3.5%.

In the tourism sector, the trend of growth of tourist arrivals and nights continued. Tourists are excited to visit many places in Montenegro like it is shown in Exhibits 5, 6, and 7.

Exhibit 5 One of the Islands in Boka Kotor Bay. Source: National Touristic Community (NTC) of Montenegro

Exhibit 6 Bridge on river Tara. Source: National Touristic Community (NTC) of Montenegro

In 2016, Montenegro visited 1.8 million tourists, which is 5.9% more than in the previous year. What the number of foreign tourist arrivals amounted to is 1.7 million. In total, 11.3 million overnight stays were registered, which is 1.8% more than in 2015. Construction in 2016 registered a significant increase in the value of completed construction works of 31.5% and an increase in the effective working hours of 16.7% compared to 2015.

In 2016, the banking sector was stable. A high level of liquid assets, the growth of deposits and new loans, as well as recapitalization of some banks additionally contributed to the stability of the banking system.

The budget deficit at the end of 2016 was estimated at 129.4 million euros or 3.4% of the GDP, which is the consequence of the application of fiscal adjustment measures, as well as less realization of the capital budget from planned and higher revenue collection. The budget deficit consequently increases the net public debt, which at the end of 2016 amounted to 2.5 billion euros, out of which 2 billion euros

Exhibit 7 Mamula Island. Source: National Touristic Community (NTC) of Montenegro

were on the external debt. Also, the number of guarantees issued (foreign and domestic) amounted to 344.9 million euros. Public debt tends to grow and, therefore, difficulty in locating the source for its repayment. The current account deficit in 2016 amounted to 715 million euros or 48.1% more compared to 2015.

Total exports of goods amounted to 345.3 million euros, an increase of 6.2%. The most significant impact on export growth had an increase in exports of minerals and electricity. The total imports of goods are amounted to 2 billion euros and were 12% higher than in 2015. This primarily resulted in an increase in imports machinery and transport devices and metal products. Coverage of foreign trade deficit, the surplus realized on other current account accounts, was 56.9%, which is 10.2% points less than in the same period of the previous year.

The number of employees in 2016 amounted to 177,908 on the average, and it was higher by 1.3% compared to the average number of employees in the previous year. The total number of employees in December 2016 was 177,473, which is 2.9% higher than the number of employees in December 2015. The unemployment rate according to the Employment Agency of Montenegro, in December 2016, was 21.33% and it was higher by 4.09% in comparison with the same period of 2015. According to the Central Bank of Montenegro, GDP growth will range from 3.25 to 3.8% with a central tendency of around 3.6% in 2017.

According to IPER (2017), there are some entrepreneurial activities alive. These are related to energy sector, agriculture, tourism, and women entrepreneurship, sponsored by the European Bank for Reconstruction and Development (EBRD) and the European Union Funds (EU Funds).

4 Toward the Future

Montenegro as a small country in the region of ex-Yugoslavia has its own challenges, issues, and problems like many other Balkan economies in transitions (Ramadani and Schneider 2013). However, it has an advantage of its geo-strategic location on the Balkan Peninsula.

Being under one system (socialist communism) and transiting to another is a challenging task. Not only economic issues become barriers, but other political, cultural, and regional issues too. It was difficult to get the real independence from Serbia in the 2000s (Lukšić and Kantić 2016). It is because Serbia had a long time influence in every political and economic move of Montenegro. After its independence, Montenegro moved quickly toward EU integration process and on the scale of doing business was advancing.

Montenegro's population is not huge. It is favorable because natural resources the country has can cover up its internal economic activities and gain a surplus. Hence, entrepreneurship development should be at much better level.

The multicultural environment in Montenegro can bring important values to its social and economic development across the country. Although multi-ethnicity and Yugopluralist model happened to be disadvantaged in some sense (Dana 2010), Montenegro can use it as an advantage by which the state can create a good business networking in ex-Yugoslavia region. Montenegro is like other ex-Yugoslavian republics, with "specific country factors" (Palalic 2017; Palalic et al. 2017) (multicultural and multi-religious environment), which sometimes prevent entrepreneurship development and do not allow its smooth flow that will bring new values for the socioeconomic development of the country.

Taking into consideration of all resources that Montenegro possesses, it has potentials for the local and foreign entrepreneurship development. All Montenegrins believe in a better future for their successor much better than they live it now.

5 Case Study: ŠAJO GROUP[3]

Mr. Žarko Rakčević is a cofounder of Šajo system in Montenegro. Mr. Rakčević is in his early 50s; he is married with three kids. Two of them already university degree holders in business and economics, and the youngest one is still a high school first grade. Mr. Rakčević has also Bachelor in Economics and Master in Tourism

---

[3]This case is written by Ramo Palalić based on interview with the company's owner.

Management. Very close to the dissolution of Yugoslavia, he has submitted his Ph.D. proposal at the University of Podgorica in the field of Tourism Management. However, due to all happenings in the 1990s, he was not able to complete it. Apart from this, he was very enthusiastic, very energetic, and active young man in his environment, and he was President of the Committee of Yugoslavian Youth for Science and Technology.

The milestone of this system was his father who was a civil engineer and still doing a great job in the group. As a shadow man, his great experience was the tremendous contribution to starting a big system like it is now.

As a young entrepreneur in his 28s, Mr. Žarko Rakčević followed steps of his father and started his first entrepreneurial activities. First transactions happened in his early age with products from his garden what his father has produced. Mr. Rakčević says:

> I learned at that time what does mean demand and supply! I learned what marketing is...when you put the most beautiful peach on the top to attract consumers...I learned what does mean a good location, price!

His first experience has got in their local bazar in Podgorica. Very soon, Mr. Rakčević ran a bakery business in Podgorica. Everyone was surprised since he was a promising young man[4] who should contribute to the science, education, and even politics, instead of opening a small startup like a bakery. However, he was fortitudinous enough to overcome these kinds of complexes that many people had. It is because, in the Yugoslavian time, entrepreneurs were considered as rebellions of the system. Conversely, persons who were close to the political system were very much appreciated and the promising ones in the society.

In the Šajo group, there are *construction, milling, tourism*, and *sales* business activities. The *construction* was the first entrepreneurial activity. They recognized an opportunity to start with building flats for local citizens on their inherited land. An advantage of the business was the experience that Mr. Rakčević's father had.

Milling was another opportunity that was recognized as a gap in the Montenegrin market. In 2003, milling at that time was in a critical state and had to be updated. They were three in Montenegro but not in full use. They observed that the technology is outdated and new machinery should be bought. They did it. Introducing a new technology in this business, it contributed to increase of agriculture business across Montenegro. Nowadays, it is still working and brings values to the *Šajo Group* and the society.

The third component of the system is *tourism*, which consists of several hotels. A small hotel in Podgorica has 22 rooms with 50 beds. Another hotel in Herceg Novi has 40 apartments with 120 beds. *Šajo Group* has bought a hotel in 2006 (*Hotel Vile Oliva*) in Petrovac in the joint consortium. The hotel counts 274 rooms and apartments with 700 beds (Exhibit 8, 9 and 10).

---

[4]A promising man is the one who has a lot of savvy to hold public, political economic or other positions and who was recognized as that in their society. That was very common in ex-Yugoslavia.

Exhibit 8 Hotel Vile Oliva in Petrovac. Photo © R.Palalić

Exhibit 9 Hotel Vile Oliva in Petrovac. Photo © R.Palalić

Exhibit 10 Olive trees inside the hotel Vile Oliva in Petrovac. Photo © R.Palalić

The fourth element of the whole business is sales. This *sales* service is mainly for the internal use of the Šajo Group. It acts as a supplier to the entire system and at the same time serves as a separate business entity.

Hotel Vile Oliva is interesting, successful story. It should be noted that when it was bought, like an old hotel, it has been planned; reconstructed and all ergonomics were done by its Šajo Group expertise. The hotel had sales of only 600,000 euros and was making the loss of 150,000 euros. Once it was under the Šajo Group, it had in 2016, 1.7 million euros of net profit. It has already sold all rooms for the year 2018. Interestingly, the customers are 99% from abroad, and 1% goes to locals from Montenegro. The hotel initially was two start hotel, and after the takeover, it is promoted into four + star hotel. It has grounded well in the international market having business networks with the world-class tour companies like Thomas Cook. Additionally, it has established a business network with Nordic countries clubs and families from the Europe and Russia mainly.

When it comes to the market, Šajo Group has the competitive advantage of possessing a well-designed system within the group, which fully support each other. Moreover, their experience in construction and tourism at the same time makes this business success more unbeatable in the market. As devoted to market needs and wants, the group paves the way for long-term, positive, and profitable relationship with the current and prospective customers in the international market.

The system of the Šajo Group led by Mr. Žarko Rakčević is in the growth stage and has potentials in the long term. The Šajo Group is open for new acquisitions and expansion to a new market. The entrepreneurial leadership of this system has always been devoted to its development and satisfying customer needs and wants. Due to his passion for the business, Mr. Rakčević sees his business as one of the leaders in the Montenegro in the field of tourism.

References

Centralna Banka Crne Gore. (2016). *Godišnji makroekonomski izvještaj CBCG*. Retrieved October 30, 2017, from http://www.cb-cg.org/index.php?mn1=publikacije&mn2=godisnji_izvjestaj& mn3=godisnji_makroekonomski_izvjestaj_cbcg

Dana, L.-P. (2010). *When economies change hands: A survey of entrepreneurship in the emerging markets of Europe from the Balkans to the Baltic states*. New York: Routledge.

IPER. (2017). *Institute za preduzetništvo i ekonomski razvoj*. Retrieved November 11, 2017, from http://iper.org.me/en/

Lukšić, I., & Katnić, M. (2016). The making of a state: Transition in Montenegro. *Cato Journal, 36* (3), 689–709.

Montenegro Facts Government Guide Series. (2010). *Government of Montenegro public relations bureau*. Podgorica: Government of Montenegro.

Palalic, R. (2017). The phenomenon of entrepreneurial leadership in gazelles and mice: A qualitative study from Bosnia and Herzegovina. *World Review of Entrepreneurship Management and Sustainable Development, 13*(2–3), 211–236.

Palalic, R., Ramadani, V., & Dana, L. P. (2017). Entrepreneurship in Bosnia and Herzegovina: Focus on gender. *European Business Review, 29*(4), 476–496.

Ramadani, V., & Schneider, R. C. (2013). *Entrepreneurship in the Balkans*. Heidelberg: Springer.

Statistical Office of Montenegro—MONSTAT. (2017). *Latest news*. Retrieved October 30, 2017, from http://www.monstat.org/eng/index.php

World Bank. (2017). *Doing business report 2017*. Washington, DC: The International Bank for Reconstruction and Development/The World Bank.

Ramo Palalić is an assistant professor at the Management Program, Faculty of Business and Administration, International University of Sarajevo, Sarajevo, Bosnia and Herzegovina. His research interests are entrepreneurship, leadership, marketing, and management. He teaches at both undergraduate and postgraduate levels in the above areas. Apart from this, he is actively involved in business projects in the areas of entrepreneurial leadership and marketing management, in private and public organizations. He has authored and coauthored several articles in the reputable international journals. Currently, he is serving a few journals as reviewer/editor board member.

Azra Bičo has graduated as Bachelor of Economics at Department of Economics and Management at International University of Sarajevo in 2010, and her MA was attained in the year of 2014 at the same institution in the field of Economics as well. Azra Bičo is the author of a number of scientific papers, presented at international scientific conferences. Currently, she is working as senior assistant at Department of Economics and Management at International University of Sarajevo. She has been assisting and lecturing Macroeconomics course, Labour Economics, International Economics course, and Growth and Development. Her research interests include labour economics, macroeconomics, and gender studies in relation to Labour Economics.

Veland Ramadani is an associate professor at South-East European University, Republic of Macedonia, where he teaches both undergraduate and postgraduate courses in entrepreneurship and small business management. His research interests include entrepreneurship, small business management, and venture capital investments. He authored or coauthored around 80 research articles and 17 books. Dr. Ramadani is an associate editor of *International Journal of Entrepreneurship and Small Business (IJESB)*. Dr. Ramadani received the Award for Excellence 2015—Outstanding Reviewer by Emerald Group Publishing (*Journal of Enterprising Communities: People and Places in the Global Economy*).

Léo-Paul Dana earned BA and MBA degrees at McGill University and a PhD from HEC-Montreal. He is professor of Entrepreneurship at Montpellier Business School and a member of the Entrepreneurship & Innovation chair of LabEx Entrepreneurship (University of Montpellier, France). He formerly served as visiting professor of Entrepreneurship at INSEAD and deputy director of the International Business MBA Programme at Nanyang Business School. He has published extensively in a variety of leading journals including the *British Food Journal, Cornell Quarterly, Entrepreneurship and Regional Development, Entrepreneurship: Theory and Practice, Journal of Small Business Management, Journal of World Business,* and *Small Business Economics*. His research interests focus on cultural issues, including the internationalization of entrepreneurship.

Entrepreneurship in Serbia

Saša Petković and Maja Ivanović Đukić

Abstract Entrepreneurship development in Serbia since its creation until today has been passing throughout a number of rises and downs. An analysis of the influencing factors of economic and entrepreneurship development will be divided into three phases. The first phase is covering the period from sixth to seventh centuries when the Serbs settled the Balkan Peninsula until getting independency from the Ottoman Empire in 1878. The second phase will cover the period until the end of World War Two while the third phase will cover the period during comunism regime in the former Yugoslavia and transition period to modern Serbia. Over the past two decades, since 2000, the increasing contribution to national competitiveness of Serbia has been provided by small and medium-sized enterprises and entrepreneurs (SMEs). The subject of this chapter is the analysis of the SME sector and the business environment in Serbia and the examination of the impact of the SME sector on national competitiveness. The aim of the research is to analyze the influencing factors of the development of entrepreneurship in Serbia through its history from the sixth century to the present day. The starting assumption of the study is that the SME sector has had a significant impact on national competitiveness of Serbia. In order to verify the validity of this assumption, the relationship between the total number of SMEs (based on the data of the Business Registers Agency) and the national competitiveness of Serbia (based on the Global Competitiveness Index) in the period from 2004 to 2015 was first examined. Then we analyzed the impact of individual segments of SMEs businesses on national competitiveness in order to identify the areas of business where the link with national competitiveness was the strongest. For the analysis descriptive statistics, correlation and regression analysis have been used. It has been proven that the SMEs sector had a significant impact on Serbia's national competitiveness in the observed period and that the link between these variables was

S. Petković (✉)
University of Banja Luka, Banja Luka, Bosnia and Herzegovina
e-mail: sasa.petkovic@ef.unibl.org

M. I. Đukić
University of Niš̌, Niš, Serbia
e-mail: maja.djukic@eknfak.ni.ac.rs

© Springer International Publishing AG, part of Springer Nature 2018
R. Palalić et al. (eds.), *Entrepreneurship in Former Yugoslavia*,
https://doi.org/10.1007/978-3-319-77634-7_7

statistically significant, so that the conclusion could be generalized and same trends could be expected in the future. As the most important segments of SMEs' operations affecting national competitiveness, productivity of labor and participation of SMEs in export have been highlighted.

1 Introduction

Serbia, the former core republic of Yugoslavia, is now a landlocked country in the central part of the Balkan Peninsula in Southeastern Europe. The country covers an area of 77,474 km^2 (excluding Kosovo/UNMIK), this is about the size of the Czech Republic, or slightly smaller than the US state of South Carolina. Serbia has a population of 7.04 million people in 2017 (Statistical Office of the Republic of Serbia 2017), the capital and largest city is Belgrade (pop. 1.6 million), and official language is Serbian written in Cyrillic. Exhibit 1 shows Belgrade, the capital of Serbia.

The Republic of Serbia is a democratic state based on the rule of law and social justice, principles of civil democracy, human and minority rights and freedom, and adherence to European principles and values. Serbia pronounced its independence on June 5, 2006, as the international legal successor to the State Union of Serbia-Montenegro. The Constitution of the Republic of Serbia came into effect on November 8th, 2006 (The President of the Republic of Serbia 2017). GDP per capita, PPP (current international dollars), is $13,671.43 (World Economic Forum

Exhibit 1 Belgrade, Serbia capital; photo © 2017 Branko Birač

Exhibit 2 National symbols and anthem of the Republic of Serbia. Source: The President of the Republic of Serbia, 2017. Retrieved from http://www.predsednik.rs/en/documents/national-symbols. Accessed on July 5, 2017

2015). Global Competitiveness Index 2015–2016 ranked Serbia 94th out of 140 countries (World Economic Forum 2015). The Constitution of the Republic of Serbia establishes the following: the Republic of Serbia shall have its coat of arms, flag, and national anthem (Exhibit 2). The coat of arms is used as the large and small coat of arms. The flag is used as the national flag and the state flag. The national anthem is a nineteenth century ceremonial song "Boze Pravde" (God of Justice).

As it was a case with other European nations, the economic development in Serbia can be observed in several phases, evolutively since the beginning of settling of the Serbs to the Western Balkans in the sixth and seventh centuries, through the construction of the Serbian medieval state, the long-term slavery under the authority of the Ottoman Empire, and less and more dynamically in the period from 1878 when Serbia gained its independence to these days. In the last two centuries, Serbia has participated in numerous warfares and fought for its survival, from the Balkan wars, the First and Second World War to the last war in 1999 when Serbia was attacked by the NATO alliance. All these circumstances have influenced the creation of an economic environment, the level of development of the transport infrastructure and institutions of entrepreneurial infrastructure, the level of economic development in general, and the level of entrepreneurship development in Serbia today. Nikola Tesla and Mihajlo Pupin are some of the names of Serbian scientists and entrepreneurs who indebted the whole world with their discoveries and entrepreneurial activities and inspired many entrepreneurs today to fulfill their dreams by transforming the world and making it a better place to live. One of them is Ellon Musk, who named his fast-growing factory of electric cars Tesla in honor of the Serbian genius. The subject of this chapter is the analysis of the SME sector and the business environment in Serbia and the examination of the impact of the SME sector on national competitiveness. The aim of the research is to analyze the influencing factors of the development of entrepreneurship in Serbia through its history from the sixth century to the present. In the first part, through a historical review, we will focus on the institutional development of the economy and entrepreneurship in Serbia from the sixth century to the present day. In second part of this chapter, we will describe the environment for entrepreneurship today in Serbia. In third and fourth part, we will present the research methodology and discuss research results while last part of this chapter is dedicated to conclusions and discussions toward the future.

2   Historical Overview

The Serbs came to the Balkans, along with other South Slavic tribes, in the Great Migrations during the sixth and seventh century, and were first mentioned by the Byzantine Emperor Constantine Porphyrogenitus in the tenth century, when they were settling on the territory of today's west Serbia, east and central Bosnia and Herzegovina with the Adriatic coast between the river Cetina and lake Skadar, and in the South in the area edged by the river Lima and the mountain range Prokletije. Their main activity was agriculture; they accepted agronomy by coming to new areas while livestock breeding was developed even in their old homeland. "The new tool used for agriculture was plow. The Slavs neglected the exploitation of the mines, which at the time of the Roman Empire were exceptionally developed in the Balkans. Following crafts were developed: weaving, pottery, and carpentry" (Vučo 1955, p. 7). The oldest written records of the Serbs in the Balkans can be found in the Frankish annals from the year 822, where it is said that the Serbs are a powerful nation that holds the greater part of Dalmatia. "However, the serious spread of Serbs and the creation of an organized feudal state can only be spoken from the twelfth century in the period of Nemanjić" (Vučo 1955, p. 40).

> During the 13th century, mining was rebuilt (it was developed in the Roman era and neglected by the Slavs). This was influenced by wealthy merchants, especially from Dubrovnik. They appear in the role of a tenant. They were renting mines, exploit metals, and sell them in overseas countries where mining was not developed, and there was a demand for metals, especially precious. These are the first signs of entrepreneurship (Vučo 1955, p. 88).

With the arrival of the Nemanjić dynasty, Serbia experienced a great economic, political, as well as military prosperity; developed its legal system; won its own autocephalous church; and became an empire in the fourteenth century. Despot Stefan Lazarević, the successor and son of King Lazar who lost his life in the battle with the Turks in Kosovo on 28th June 1389, announced the "Law on Mines" on 29th January 1412 (Mihaljčić 1997; Mičeta 2015), with a special part that regulated

life in then the largest mine in the Balkans, Novo Brdo. This additionally strength-
ened the development of mining, which was the main economic branch of the Serbia
in that period of time, so that at the end of his rule, Serbia was one of the largest silver
producers in Europe (Babić-Đorđević and Đurić 1982).

> The fall of the Serbian Empire began with the death of Dušan the Mighty (about 1308-1355),
> the first Serbian emperor. Dušan's empire in various forms and volumes will be held for an
> over a century, until 1459, when the Serbian medieval state disappears from the historical
> scene by the fall of Smederevo (Mičeta 2015, p. 17).

"Until 1804, till the Great Karađorđe did not raise a cross and launched the soul of
Serbia, for 345 years, the Serbs, as the English priest Douglas said, were wearing
blackness" (Mičeta 2015, p. 17). "Serbia's commercial and cultural awakening in the
late eighteenth century had not taken place on native soil but rather among emigrants
to the Habsburg Vojvodina" (Lampe 1975, p. 31). Belgrade was Serbia's major port,
located at the confluence of the Danube and Sava just across the river from the
Habsburg Monarchy and its huge markets. "The town was already the commercial
center of the Serbian lands when it became the capital of an autonomous province in
the Ottoman Empire in 1830 (Lampe 1975, p. 35). Exhibit 3 shows Ada Belgrade, an
attractive, multifunctional zone in Belgrade.

Serbia, Greece, and Romania had achieved largely autonomous governments by
the early 1860s. They were accorded formal independence in 1878 (Lampe and
Jackson 1982). Exhibit 4 shows railway station in Niš, Serbia, 1881.

> After the Berlin Congress, there is an accelerated development of foreign trade, when
> exports become much higher than imports, and crafts, ores, and so on are becoming more
> and more involved. Most of the exports from Serbia were absorbed by Austria (partly for
> their own needs and partially for resale) (Vučo 1955, p. 228).

Exhibit 3 Ada Bridge, Belgrade; photo © 2017 Branko Birač

Exhibit 4 Railway station in Niš, Serbia, 1881. Source: Retrieved from http://niskevesti.rs/1340-na-danasnji-dan-nis-postao-najvaznija-zeleznicka-raskrsnica-na-balkanu/. Accessed on July 27, 2017

In order to stimulate the development of industry in Serbia in 1873, a law was adopted by which the capitalists (domestic and foreign) who build the factories were released from customs on imports of machinery and goods for the production purposes and some taxes, and they were given the right to use the state land and forests. "It did not produce exceptional results. By the end of the nineteenth century, there were only 28 industrial enterprises with 1702 workers, mostly small enterprises with 20 employees" (Vučo 1955, p. 248). "Construction of the railway had a great impact on the development of foreign trade. The first railway Belgrade-Nis-Vranje was built in 1881" (Vučo 1955, p. 222).

> During the Tariff War with Austria-Hungary between 1906 and 1911, the city's industry provided the import substitutes, mainly construction materials, and the exports of processed meat that constituted the economic basis of the eventual Serbian victory. Together these Belgrade manufacturers accounted for well over half the value of Serbian industrial production in 1911, with only a small fraction tied to government contracts or credit (Lampe 1975, p. 35).

In order to encourage the founding of large companies, a new law was adopted in 1898 which gives much greater privileges. The capitalists who set up large enterprises with at least 50 employees and 50,000 dinars of invested capital had a right to be a subject of exemption of all taxes, customs duties, and other charges; had a right to use state land, water from rivers and streams, ores from mines, sand, and gravel; had a right to make roads for production purposes; they could use rail transport at lower rates prices; etc. This led to significant industrial development in Serbia in the period from 1898 to 1910, when there were 428 enterprises with 16,100 employees. The most developed branches of industry were: milling, brewing, and other

Exhibit 5 The historical boundaries of Yugoslavia from 1919 to 1992. Source: Encyclopedia Britannica, Inc., 2017. Retrieved from https://www.britannica.com/place/Serbia. Accessed on July 19, 2017

industries and then the textile industry whose center was in Leskovac (Vučo 1955, p. 248) (Exhibit 5).

> In the beginning of 1920s, Serbia was an integral part of Yugoslavia (meaning "Land of the South Slavs"), which included the modern countries of Serbia, Croatia, Slovenia, Bosnia and Herzegovina, Kosovo, Macedonia, and Montenegro. Long ruled by the Ottoman Empire and Austria-Hungary, these component nations combined in 1918 to form an independent federation known as the Kingdom of Serbs, Croats, and Slovenes. In 1929, that federation was formally constituted as Yugoslavia. Serbia was the dominant part in this multiethnic union, though after World War II the nonaligned communist government of Josip Broz Tito accorded some measure of autonomy to the constituent republics and attempted to balance contending interests by dividing national administrative responsibilities (e.g., for intelligence and defense) along ethnic lines (Allcock et al. 2017).

The Socialist Federal Republic of Yugoslavia (SFRY) was formed after the Second World War. The accelerated industrial development of the country began as well as the application of the socialist model of development, so-called Self-managing socialism. Large enterprises were created to exploit the effects of economies of scale (Ivanović-Đukić and Lepojević 2015a, b), while the development of SMEs was largely ignored (Filipović 2003).

> Until the end of the 1980s and early 1990s, the Federal Government of the SFRY began to implement measures related to the establishment of SMEs. During this period, a large number of small and medium-sized enterprises and entrepreneurs were established (Filipović 2003, p. 26).

However, a favorable climate for the development of SMEs has not continued. There was stagnation in the development of the SME sector, after the collapse of the SFRY in 1991. The state policy was again focused on supporting large systems in which the largest amount of capital and workforce was concentrated. The position of SMEs is further aggravated by the impact of unfavorable external factors such as UN sanctions and war in the environment in the former republics of the SFRY. In the former Yugoslavia, the initial stages of transition were interrupted by the wars between 1991 and 1995, which, in addition to large human casualties, had great consequences on the population, infrastructure, economy, and nonprofit activities, such as education, health, culture, and sport (Petković 2017).

Because of this, a large number of SMEs were closed, in the coming years (Ivanović-Đukić and Stefanović 2011a, b). After the political changes in 2001, the new Government understands that SMEs have great potential to create gross domestic product and to employ a large number of workers. As a result, a number of measures are being implemented in order to create a favorable business climate for the development of SMEs. This stimulates the rapid growth and development of the SME sector.

Precise records of the SMEs' number and monitoring of their resources and performance has started since 2004. For these reasons, this chapter will analyze the development of the SME sector in the period from 2004 to 2015.

3   Environment for Entrepreneurship

A large number of implemented macroeconomic measures influenced the development of the SME sector in Serbia in the late 1980s of the twentieth century (Ivanović-Đukić and Lepojević 2015a, b). The Government of Yugoslavia established the Agency for Small and Medium Enterprises and Entrepreneurship, which was the basis for further development of institutional and legislative framework. In addition, in order to improve the macroeconomic environment, the liberalization of trade regime created a legal framework for the establishment of joint stock companies and private companies. Also, a number of accompanying measures have been adopted in order to increase the competitiveness and economic efficiency of SMEs, in the period 1988–1992. As a result of these measures, a large number of private SMEs were established in a relatively short time period (Filipović 2003).

> There were 20,443 SMEs in Serbia in 1990. The largest expansion of registered companies in Serbia was in the period 1990–1994. Then the number of registered companies was increased by almost 180,000 (from 25,173 in 1990 to 202,943 in 1994). The highest average annual increase was recorded in the period 1991–1993. And it amounted to 9530 private companies. . .The number of SMEs in Serbia was increased to 180,431 and 176,724 entrepreneurs by 2000. The largest number of SMEs was in the field of trade (47%), while in the field of industry and mining, only 12% of SMEs operated. The largest number of entrepreneurs was concentrated in the field of trade (28.7%) and crafts (27.0%), while in the field of industry and mining there were only 3.6% of entrepreneurs. The number of employees in SMEs increased significantly (from around 400 thousand to around 1.35 million) in the 10-year period (1990–2000) (Chamber of Commerce 2015, pp. 2–10).

However, the rapid growth of the number of SMEs in the period 1990–2000 should be tied to a very low starting point. In addition, the lack of a comprehensive and consistent policy and program of measures to encourage and support the development of SMEs in the period from 1990 to 2000 resulted in their concentration in services and trade sector with low numbers of employees and low value of own capital. There is no significant manifestation of entrepreneurial initiatives in production sector due to lack of capital for the development of SMEs and unfavorable and changing business conditions. In such an environment, the development of the private sector SMEs was generally modest. Regardless of all the weaknesses and problems noted, SMEs were the only economic structure that in that period consistently achieved positive business results. SMEs accounted for around 40% of the country's GDP and employed around 800,000 workers, with a relatively small share of capital of only 6%. The great development potential of this sector was noticed and a comprehensive reform in the direction of its development was underway (Chamber of Commerce 2015). Many studies have shown that the developed countries that encouraged entrepreneurship and SMEs development had a higher economic growth (Audretsch and Thurik 2000; Ács and Naudé 2013; Naudé 2013). Entrepreneurship is also linked to the development of developing countries, considering entrepreneurial activity as an important driver of economic growth in these countries (Audretsch et al. 2006; Van Praag and Versloot 2007).

Understanding the importance of SMEs, the state has begun implementing systemic measures since 2003, to encourage their development into three following segments:

- In creation of developing policies (laws and strategies)
- In developing a support institution (business incubators, clusters, technology centers, industrial zones, etc.)
- In developing the direct programs of financial support (grants, loans, etc.) and various forms of nonfinancial assistance (training, information, counseling, etc.).

All three forms of SME incentives were implemented at different levels: republic, provincial, and local.

The most frequently used incentive measures for the development of SMEs were:

- Support for research and development, innovation, and technology development.
- Encouraging SMEs in underdeveloped areas.
- Help in start-up.
- Development of all elements of business infrastructure that should provide assistance to SMEs located at different development levels.
- The development of financial institutions and financial products tailored to the financing of SMEs.
- Encouraging the connection between SMEs (clusters, etc.) (Filipović 2003, p. 28).

The implementation of these measures has led to the accelerated growth and development of SME sector. At the same time, the implementation of new measures continues. In January 2003, the government of the Republic of Serbia adopted the Strategy for the Development of Small and Medium Enterprises and Entrepreneurship in the Republic of Serbia for the period 2003–2008. The strategy was a basic document defining the direction of the future Government's activities in order to create a favorable environment and support the development of SME sector. The main aim of the strategy was to create a framework for creating a sustainable, internationally competitive, and export-oriented SME sector. Two priority tasks of the strategy were: increasing the total number of SMEs as well as increasing number of employees in the SME sector. The implementation of this strategy implied a lot of measures which have been taken toward the creation of stimulating environment for the development of SMEs. First of all, large number of regulations was adopted in order to eliminate legal and administrative barriers. Also, a number of institutions have been established to provide support in solving financing problems. Unfortunately, the expected results have not been achieved.

The World Economic Crisis, which caused deep disturbances in the global market, had great negative effects on achieved results of SME. These disorders affected financial and economic flows in the Republic of Serbia and had negative influence on all business entities, including SMEs. The business environment for SMEs in the Republic of Serbia has become considerably less favorable since 2009 compared to the previous few years, due to the effects of the global crisis (Ivanović-Đukić and Lazić 2014). There was a breakdown in economic growth, and the gross domestic product of the country declined year by year, due to which the state approved a smaller amount of financial incentives for SMEs (Stefanović et al. 2013). Also, major changes occurred in the labor market. There is a decrease in the total number of employees, the growth of the unemployment rate, and the fall in average earnings. Due to the increase in the unemployment of the domestic population, the demand for products and services of SMEs (which mainly operate on the national market) has been decreasing, so their volume of business has decreased and their growth has slowed down (Bošnjak 2011). Also, there was less money and capital in the country, due to the difficult conditions for attracting foreign investments. The liquidity of business entities is reduced, due to which the accounts of many SMEs have become blocked, and many of them are closed. All this follows the inflation rate of over 10% (Bošnjak 2011). These and a large number of other macroeconomic factors with a large number of internal ones have led to large oscillations of the number of SMEs in the period from 2004 to 2015, which can be seen from Table 1.

The number of SMEs has increased significantly in the period from 2004 (88,682) to 2015 (109,118). At the same time, the number of employees in SME increased (from 682,349 in 2004 to 735,007 in 2015). This can be seen from Table 2.

The increase in the number of SMEs, accompanied by an increase in the number of employees in them, points to the development of this sector in Serbia. The same tendencies also show movements in the value of the assets and capital of that group of economic entities. This can be seen from Tables 3 and 4.

It is obvious that the value of the assets of SMEs is constantly increasing in the period from 2004 to 2013, when there was a slight decrease. Oscillations in capital during the observed period are much higher. There is a significant increase in capital in each group of business entities in 2015.

For monitoring growth and development of SMEs sector, indicators of business success of SMEs in Serbia are very important. For the purposes of analyzing business success of entrepreneurs and SMES, changing trends of achieved performances (revenue and profit) in the observed period can be tracked, which is shown in the Tables 5 and 6.

Table 1 Comparative overview of the number of small and medium-sized enterprises and entrepreneurs in Serbia in the period from 2004 to 2015

Year	Entrepreneurs	Small enterprises	Medium enterprise	Total number of SME
2004	13,464	73,097	2121	88,682
2005	19,987	72,888	2288	95,163
2006	21,584	73,549	2412	97,545
2007	22,285	80,671	3078	106,034
2008	22,066	85,389	3520	110,975
2009	21,899	85,198	3499	110,596
2010	21,262	87,284	2870	111,416
2011	20,500	88,306	2751	111,557
2012	19,679	88,354	2866	110,899
2013	18,974	90,597	2846	112,417
2014	18,204	94,746	2131	115,081
2015	17,282	89,653	2182	109,118

Source: Macroeconomic announcements of SBRA 2004–2015. Retrieved from http://www.apr. gov.rs/Registri/Finansijskiizveštajiibonitet/Makroekonomskasaopštenja.aspx. Accessed on June 1, 2017

Table 2 Movement of the number of employees in small and medium-sized enterprises and entrepreneurs in Serbia in the period from 2004 to 2015

Year	Entrepreneurs	Small enterprises	Medium enterprise	Total number of SME
2004	28,908	388,906	264,535	682,349
2005	41,409	360,992	256,460	658,861
2006	46,969	386,296	253,898	687,163
2007	50,806	382,168	257,996	690,970
2008	52,590	386,005	260,409	699,004
2009	49,872	365,788	242,565	658,225
2010	45,098	362,306	219,456	626,860
2011	45,099	372,573	213,591	631,263
2012	43,995	363,285	207,936	615,216
2013	43,350	356,699	205,916	605,965
2014	43,025	461,623	220,944	725,592
2015	45,545	490,956	198,506	735,007

Source: Macroeconomic announcements of SBRA 2004–2015. Retrieved from http://www.apr. gov.rs/Registri/Finansijskiizveštajiibonitet/Makroekonomskasaopštenja.aspx. Accessed on June 1, 2017

It is obvious that results achieved by the SMEs increased with certain oscillations in the period from 2004 to 2015. Negative tendencies were present in the period from 2009 to 2012 under the influence of the global economic crisis. However, business results have had continuously high growth rates since 2013. These tendencies point to the fact that there was an increase in the number of SMEs (growth of SME sector), which was accompanied by the improvement of their business, in the period from 2004 to 2015.

Table 3 Assets of SMEs and entrepreneurs in Serbia in the period from 2004 to 2015 (000.000 RSD)

Year	Entrepreneurs	Small enterprises	Medium enterprise	Total number of SME
2004	26,131	964,825	725,851	1,716,807
2005	48,928	861,781	703,371	1,614,080
2006	62,546	1,493,142	1,039,865	2,595,553
2007	75,131	1,009,907	1,275,163	2,360,201
2008	87,316	1,715,079	1,929,367	3,731,762
2009	87,446	1,738,036	1,967,135	3,792,617
2010	92,174	2,715,500	1,752,312	4,559,986
2011	97,861	2,834,907	1,810,865	4,743,633
2012	100,005	3,689,249	1,842,834	5,633,037
2013	96,554	3,663,035	2,104,300	5,863,889
2014	93,013	2,306,469	1,952,369	4,351,851
2015	98,489	2,315,622	2,152,540	4,566,651

Source: Macroeconomic announcements of SBRA 2004–2015. Retrieved from http://www.apr. gov.rs/Registri/Finansijskiizveštajiibonitet/Makroekonomskasaopštenja.aspx. Accessed on June 1, 2017

Table 4 Capital of SMEs and entrepreneurs in Serbia in the period from 2004 to 2015 (000.000 RSD)

Year	Entrepreneurs	Small enterprises	Medium enterprise	Total number of SMEs
2004	9723	322,259	378,739	710,721
2005	17,616	404,467	418,266	840,349
2006	19,951	549,642	509,842	1,079,435
2007	21,961	479,296	730,955	1,232,212
2008	22,600	550,081	782,655	1,355,335
2009	21,866	600,138	813,322	1,435,326
2010	22,654	928,696	660,987	1,612,337
2011	24,687	1,049,866	713,997	1,788,550
2012	25,156	1,331,671	721,856	2,078,683
2013	24,703	1,302,579	789,093	2,116,375
2014	26,514	949,830	797,174	1,773,518
2015	30,499	978,465	909,609	1,918,573

Source: Macroeconomic announcements of SBRA 2004–2015. Retrieved from http://www.apr. gov.rs/Registri/Finansijskiizveštajiibonitet/Makroekonomskasaopštenja.aspx. Accessed on June 1, 2017

3.1 Research Methodology, Research Model, and Hypotheses

According to Stel et al. (2005), research shows that, in recent years, an increasing importance for achieving economic growth and improving the competitiveness of modern economies stands in creation and development of SMEs. Moreover, Audretsch and Thurik (2001) claim that the most competitive countries have had

Table 5 Business performances of entrepreneurs and small enterprises in the period 2004–2015 (in 000.000 RSD)

	Entrepreneurs			Small enterprises		
Year	Total revenue	Total expenditures	Profit	Total revenue	Total expenditures	Profit
2004	56,353	54,472	1881	1,057,153.5	1,050,643	6510.418
2005	118,809	113,451	5358	1,146,074.9	1,126,323	19,751.93
2006	152,626	147,515	5111	1,529,494	1,470,880	58,613.89
2007	171,287	165,715	5572	1,213,596.1	1,170,143	43,453.09
2008	192,990	187,988	5002	1,733,801.5	1,691,436	42,365.44
2009	179,163	175,584	3579	1,565,772.6	1,553,843	11,929.57
2010	185,749	182,557	3192	1,804,015	1,834,614	−30,599
2011	202,671	198,089	4582	2,085,040.4	2,071,454	13,585.9
2012	213,908	209,023	4885	2,126,485.8	2,159,873	−33,386.9
2013	211,172	205,666	5506	2,061,160.1	2,064,985	−3824.89
2014	202,954	196,402	6552	2,112,621	2,079,584	33,037
2015	214,522	206,197	8325	2,239,782	2,165,564	74,218

Source: Macroeconomic announcements of SBRA 2004–2015. Retrieved from http://www.apr. gov.rs/Registri/Finansijskiizveštajiibonitet/Makroekonomskasaopštenja.aspx. Accessed on June 1, 2017

Table 6 Business performances of medium-sized enterprises and SME sector in Serbia in the period 2004–2015 (in 000.000 RSD)

	Medium-sized enterprises			SME sector		
Year	Total revenue	Total expenditures	Profit	Total revenue	Total expenditures	Profit
2004	595,191	613,649	−18,458	1,708,698	1,718,764	−10,066.8
2005	636,886	642,960	−6073.3	1,901,770	1,882,734	19,036.61
2006	850,776	837,576	13,200	2,532,896	2,455,971	76,924.89
2007	1,187,943	906,016	281,928	2,572,827	2,241,874	330,953
2008	1,371,817	1,368,431	3385.97	3,298,608	3,247,855	50,753.42
2009	1,235,836	1,259,431	−23,594	2,980,772	2,988,858	−8085.46
2010	1,317,762	1,322,969	−5207.3	3,307,526	3,340,140	−32,614.3
2011	1,427,834	1,413,058	14,776.2	3,715,545	3,682,601	32,944.11
2012	1,545,541	1,530,526	15,014.9	3,885,935	3,899,422	−13,487
2013	1,541,100	1,525,084	16,016	3,813,432	3,795,735	17,697.11
2014	1,724,125	1,735,613	−11,488	4,039,700	4,011,599	28,101
2015	1,842,858	1,788,567	54,291	4,082,640	3,954,131	128,509

Source: Macroeconomic announcements of SBRA 2004–2015. Retrieved from http://www.apr. gov.rs/Registri/Finansijskiizveštajiibonitet/Makroekonomskasaopštenja.aspx. Accessed on June 1, 2017

the transition from the model of "managed economy" (based on the exploitation of economies of scale and mass production) to the model of "entrepreneurial econo-mies" (based on entrepreneurial capabilities that enable knowledge and capital overflows toward exploiting market advantages). Except them, a large number of modern economists (Acs and Audretsch 2003; Audretsch and Keilbach 2004) accept the idea of Schumpeter (1934) about entrepreneurship as the main engine of economic growth and an important source of competitiveness. Accordingly, Salgado-Banda (2007) explain Schumpeter's concept of creative destruction as a competitive process in which entrepreneurs continually search for new ideas that lead to increased resource efficiency use, due to which simultaneously existing business concepts seem old-fashioned and are being ejected from the market, after which a new productive form of business that leads to economic growth and improving national competitiveness remains in economy.

Schumpeter's assumptions may be linked to the World Economic Forum claims which in analyzing of the competitiveness give the highest relative importance to the innovation subindex within the technology in most developed countries, with the explanation that the development of new technologies based on innovation is crucial for the competitiveness of developed countries (Schwab 2014). Due to the fact that entrepreneurs (either individuals or as part of existing companies) are a significant source of new ideas and innovations, an entrepreneurial activity can be considered as a significant promoter of competitive advantage.

Also, a large number of empirical researches confirm that in developed countries, entrepreneurship has an important contribution to the economic development and national competitiveness. In developed countries, a number of studies have been conducted on the relationship between entrepreneurship and national competitiveness. Thus, for example, a study of 13 developed European countries, conducted by Carree and Thurik (1998), points to the fact that the economies with greater share of entrepreneurial activities have higher growth rates, compared to the ones with a smaller share of entrepreneurial activities. In subsequent studies (Carree and Thurik 2003; Carree et al. 2005), the same researchers prove that entrepreneurial activity contributes to increasing economic productivity and improving national competitiveness. Also, Acs and Varga (2005) find that entrepreneurship has a positive and statistically significant impact on national competitiveness, due to the effect of knowledge spillover, which is generated during growth. Wong et al. (2005) point to similar conclusions, claiming that business creativity and innovation, characteristic of SMEs, have great significance for the national competitiveness in developed countries. Naudé (2008) proves that entrepreneurship has a positive impact on the economy, because it contributes to increasing employment and intensifying competition. Valliere and Peterson (2009), based on a sample of 24 developed countries, prove that there is a positive and statistically significant correlation between entrepreneurship and national competitiveness in developed countries. It should be noted here that a large number of studies show that the largest contribution to the national competitiveness in developed countries comes from fast growing companies, the so-called gazelles, i.e., high-growth expectation entrepreneurship (Harrison 1994; Wong et al. 2005; Moreno and Casillas 2007; Valliere and Peterson 2009).

When it comes to developing countries and transition economies, there are also some scholarly articles, pointing to the importance of SME for the national competitiveness (Ivanović-Đukić and Lepojević 2014). Entrepreneurship is important for transition economies because it encourages economic development by creating an open competitive market (Megginson and Netter 2001) and contributes to limiting the market power of public enterprises (McMillian and Woodruff 2002). The particular importance of SMEs in developing countries lies in the fact that they are very dynamic, quick to learn, and rapidly change (Čučković and Bartlett 2007), which increases their competitiveness, as well as the competitiveness of the entire economy (Carlin et al. 2001).

However, although there are a large number of papers, which, based on substantiated theoretical explanations, prove the importance of entrepreneurship for national competitiveness, solid empirical evidence that this bond is present and significant is still missing. Therefore, the relationship between SMEs and national competitiveness in the case of Serbia will be examined in this chapter. Our initial assumptions were:

H_1: There is a statistically significant correlation between national competitiveness of Serbia and development of SME sector.

H_2: Development of SME sector significantly impacted national competitiveness of Serbia, under the conditions of prolonged impact of the effects of the world economic crisis.

First, the influence of development of the SME sector on the national competitiveness of Serbia in the period from 2004 to 2015 will be examined, by applying the methods of descriptive statistics, correlation, and regression. The analysis will be carried out for a period of 12 years. The analysis for 2016 cannot be carried out because there is still no available data on SME sector in Serbia for that year.

The Index of Global Competitiveness of Serbia will be used as an indicator of the national competitiveness of Serbia according to the data of the World Economic Forum. Data of the Business Registers Agency in Serbia will be used for monitoring growth of SME sector (the number of SMEs, the number of employees in them, the movement of their assets and capital, and the financial result) in the period from 2004 to 2015. The dependent variable will be the rank of Serbia's national competitiveness over the years. All other variables will have the role of an independent.

A correlation analysis will be applied in order to verify link between the development of the SME sector and national competitiveness. A regression analysis will be undertaken to check the impact of SMEs on national competitiveness. The variables which will be used in this chapter are shown in Table 7.

3.2 Research Results and Discussion

First, the average values of all variables and standard deviations from the average are calculated. The obtained results are shown in Table 8.

Table 8 shows that there were no significant deviations from the mean values for any of the observed events. More specifically, the median national competitiveness of Serbia in the period from 2004 to 2015 is 92.5 positions, the average deviation from this value over the years were 5.27. The mean value of the number of SMEs in the same period was 107,455 with an average deviation of 6415.21. The average number of employees in SMEs was 661.411 while the deviation amounted to 37,421. The average value of the funds of SMEs was 3925.300.000.000 RSD

Table 7 Variables used in the study

Variable	Abbreviations	Indicator
National competitiveness	NC	Global competitiveness index (rang)
Development of the SME sector	N	Number of SME
	NE	Number of employees
	A	Assets of SME
	C	Capital of SME
	P	Profit of SME

Table 8 Descriptive statistics

	Average	Standard deviation
National competitiveness	92.50	5.27
Number of SMEs	107,455.20	6415.21
Number of employees in SME	661,411.10	37,421.33
Assets of SME	3,925,300,000,000	1.38
Capital of SME	1,533,100,000,000	4.21
Profit of SME	50,222,443,300	1.11

Source: Calculation of authors in SPSS 17 on the basis of data obtained from macroeconomic announcements of SBRA 2004–2015

(Serbian dinars), while the average deviation was 1.38. The average value of capital was 1533.100.000.000 RSD, while the average deviation was 4.21. The average value of the achieved results was 50,222.443.300 dinars while the average deviation was 1.11.

The link between Serbia's national competitiveness and the development of the SME sector is examined by applying correlation analysis. The obtained results of the correlation analysis are shown in Table 9.

There is a strong and statistically significant indirect correlation between national competitiveness and assets (−0.813) and capital (−0.799) held by SMEs. The correlation between the national competitiveness of Serbia and number of SMEs (−0.596) and the number of employees in SMEs (−0.687) are also statistically significant and indirect, but slightly weaker compared to the previous relationship. In other words, the increase in each of the above categories leads to a decrease in Serbia's rank in the list of countries whose competitiveness is being tested, i.e., to improving its competitiveness. The results showed that the correlation is weak (0.228), between the profit of SMEs and national competitiveness. In addition, this correlation is not statistically significant.

In order to check the impact of each of the observed phenomena on national competitiveness, a regression analysis was applied. The variables profit of SME and capital of SME are excluded from the model, because they lead to multicollinearity. Confirmation of this statement on the presence of multicollinearity in data is found if we perform the diagnostic procedure for collinearity. Namely, the values of the corresponding Tolerance and VIF indicators indicate the presence of multicollinearity

Table 9 Correlation between national competitiveness and the development of the SME sector in Serbia in period 2014–2015

	Global competitiveness index	Number of SME	Number of employees in SME	Assets of SME	Capital of SME	Profit of SME
Global competitiveness index (rang)	1	−0.596 (0.023)	−0.687 (0.029)	−0.813 (0.003)	−0.799 (0.001)	−0.228 (0.612)
Number of SME		1	0.256 (0.457)	0.824 (0.003)	0.825 (0.003)	−0.217 (0.427)
Number of employees in SME			1	0.527 (0.055)	0.636 (0.079)	0.460 (0.175)
Assets of SME				1	0.996 (0.000)	0.495 (0.144)
Capital of SME					1	0.346 (0.128)
Profit of SME						1

Source: Calculation of authors in SPSS 17 on the basis of data obtained from macroeconomic announcements of SBRA 2004–2015

Table 10 Influence of SME development in Serbia on National competitiveness in the period 2004–2015 regression coefficients

	Unstandardized coefficients B	Standardized coefficients B	Significance
(Constant)	95.939		0.012
Number of SME	−0.009	−0.257	0.156
Number of employees in SME	−4.298	−0.293	0.286
Capital of SME	−7.154	−0.577	0.034
Adjusted R^2	0.688		

Source: Calculation of authors in SPSS 17 on the basis of data obtained from macroeconomic announcements of SBRA 2004–2015

in variables. By excluding these variables, we solve the problem. The results of the regression analysis are shown in Table 10.

Table 10 shows that the SME capital has the biggest impact on Serbia's national competitiveness (−0.577). An increase in the capital of SMEs for 1,000,000 RSD leads to the improvement of Serbia's Global competitiveness rank by 0.7148. Impact of other indicators is not statistically significant. The coefficient of determination R 0.688 indicates that the model is representative. The mentioned variables are influenced by 68.8% of the changes in national competitiveness.

4 Toward the Future

The chapter shows that SMEs have had an increasing importance for the development of Serbia's economy and its national competitiveness in recent years. They employ a large number of workers, have a significant share in the gross domestic product (GDP), and lead to the improvement of national competitiveness. Serbian government understood the importance of the SMEs, after the political changes in 2001. A large number of measures have been implemented toward the development of this sector of the economy since this period (since 2001). The implementation of these measures has significantly contributed to the development of the SMEs in Serbia.

Our research, based on the data of the Agency for Business Registers, showed that there was progressive growth of the SME sector (measured by the number of SMEs), the number of employees in them, the growth in the value of assets and capital in period from 2004 to 2008, but after that (in the period since 2008), the growth of the SME sector has been gradually slowing down, under the influence of the global economic crisis. Revival and development of the SME sector has started again since 2013. It is interesting that there was an increase in SME export orientation, which resulted in an increase in the value of sales revenues from foreign markets in total turnover. Our research has shown that development of SME sector in Serbia positively affects national competitiveness. The correlation between the observed phenomena is statistically significant, so the conclusion can be generalized, and similar trends can be expected in the future.

It can be suggested to macroeconomic policy makers to implement many different measures in order to stimulate future development of the SME sector and enhance national competitiveness of Serbia in the future. First of all, it is necessary to implement measures for increasing the population ability to monitor trends in environment and recognize the chances for starting a new business. This can be achieved with a greater degree of theoretical and practical knowledge involvement in educational school programs at all levels of education, by organizing various forms of education and training (through formal education programs, etc.) and by the creation of modern universities oriented to the economy and scientific research, the so-called Entrepreneurial universities. Universities around the world also play third role. The role of an entrepreneurial university, along with traditional roles as education centers and research centers (Commission of the European Communities, 2007 as state Iglesias-Sánchez et al. 2016). Logical interpretation of the so-called entrepreneurial university refers to the development of university infrastructure necessary to help students when starting their own business. We consider the entrepreneurial infrastructure in universities as organizational and sub-organizational units established to provide entrepreneurial support to students, such as business incubators, business accelerators, centers for project management, career centers, centers for technology transfer and commercialization of innovations, etc. Recent research suggests that entrepreneurial skills and attitudes can be gained through business simulation experiences (Arias-Aranda and Bustinza-Sanchez 2009).

Also, it is desirable to implement measures aimed at encouraging innovative entrepreneurial activity, because this form of entrepreneurship is the largest contributor to competitiveness in developed countries. This can be achieved by better linking the SME sector with universities and research centers in order to transfer knowledge, ideas, and other results obtained in these institutions which entrepreneurs can use to obtain new products and services. This can be achieved by encouraging development of clusters, innovation centers, high-tech incubators, etc. Since a significant contribution to GCI promotion in developed countries has IO, it can be suggested to macroeconomic policy makers in developing countries to secure various incentives and to provide other forms of assistance for entrepreneurs for entering the foreign markets and for the international orientation development.

5 Case Study: Winery Aleksic, Serbia

The Aleksic Winery is a small family firm in the south of Serbia, which is growing very fast. The core business of the firm is the production and sale of wines. It was established in 2013 by transforming the wine cellar Aleksic into a small enterprise. The founders of the Aleksic Winery are three sisters Aleksic: Dragana, Maja, and Marija (Exhibit 6). They have succeeded in transforming a small entrepreneur wine cellar into a fast-growing company, thanks to the enormous enthusiasm, energy, and dedication, with the financial support of the family. The Aleksic Winery has become a leader in the Serbian market and a remarkable brand in the European market.

The Aleksic Winery has huge vineyard areas located in the southern Serbia and the most modern equipment for the production of wine. This company offers products of excellent quality which won numerous awards and recognitions (Exhibit 7) in the country and abroad, such as: "Best Serbia producer of the year 2015" (awarded by AWAC from Vienna), the award for the best local brand in 2016, the gold medal for the quality of the wine "Bonaca limited" at the Vienna competition, the silver medal for the "Barbara" pink wine and the "Arno" in Sofia, the bronze medal for the wine "Kardash" in London, etc.

The Aleksic Winery was founded as a small family company. First, it offered products only on the local market. The expansion in the national market as well as the entry into the markets of neighboring countries has begun very quickly. Products of The Aleksic Winery are now present in the markets of a large number of EU countries, and in 2017 it is planned to enter the Russian and the US markets. Thanks to the acquisition of foreign markets and increased participation in the domestic market, the company has recorded extremely high growth rates and achieved a huge return on investments.

The Winery is going to continue with the development of its business in the future. The Winery purchased the business facilities (which it had previously leased) in the first half of 2017 and obtained a concession to use 68 ha of vineyards, which allowed it to start branding wines with the geographical origin. The branding of wines with the geographical origin is very important for increasing the participation in the European market where it is present, as well as for the expansion to new

Exhibit 6 Founders and owners of the Aleksic Winery, photo © 2017 Maja Aleksic-Ilic

Exhibit 7 Awarding at the Summit of Entrepreneurs in Dubrovnik in 2016, photo © 2017 Maja Aleksic-Ilic

markets abroad. The expansion of production capacities is also planned as well as building of a tourist facility in the vineyard. The implementation of the planned activities with the continuous growth of market share promises further development of the mentioned company and improvement of its competitiveness, as well as the increase of competitiveness of the region in which it is located.

References

Acs, Z. J., & Audretsch, D. B. (2003). Innovation and technological change. In Z. J. Acs & D. B. Audretsch (Eds.), *Handbook of entrepreneurship research*. Boston: Kluwer Academic Publishers.

Ács, Z. J., & Naudé, W. A. (2013). Entrepreneurship, stages of development and industrialization. In A. Szirmai, W. A. Naudé, & L. Alcorta (Eds.), *Pathways to industrialization in the 21st Century* (pp. 373–392). Oxford: Oxford University Press.

Acs, Z. J., & Varga, A. (2005). Entrepreneurship, agglomeration and technological change. *Small Business Economics, 24*(3), 323–334. https://doi.org/10.1007/s11187-005-1998-4

Allcock, J. B., Lampe, J. R., & Poulsen, T. M. (2017). *Serbia*. Retrieved from https://www.britannica.com/place/Serbia

Arias-Aranda, D., & Bustinza-Sánchez, O. (2009). Entrepreneurial attitude and conflict management through business simulations. *Industrial Management & Data Systems, 109*(8), 1101–1117. https://doi.org/10.1108/02635570910991328

Audretsch, D., & Thurik, A. (2000). Capitalism and democracy in the 21st century: From the managed to the entrepreneurial economy. *Journal of Evolutionary Economics, 10*(1), 17–34. https://doi.org/10.1007/s001910050003

Audretsch, D. B., & Keilbach, M. (2004). Entrepreneurship capital and economic performance. *Regional Studies, 28*(5), 949–959. https://doi.org/10.1080/0034340042000280956

Audretsch, D. B., Ketlbach, M. C., & Lehmann, E. E. (2006). *Entrepreneurship and economic growth*. Oxford: Oxford University Press.

Audretsch, D. B., & Thurik, A. R. (2001). What is new about the new economy: Sources of growth in the growth in the managed and entrepreneurial economies. *Industrial and Corporate Change, 10*(1), 267–315. https://doi.org/10.1093/icc/10.1.267

Babić-Đorđević, G., & Đurić, V. J. (1982). *Polet umetnosti. Istorija srpskog naroda. knj. 2*. Beograd: Srpska književna zadruga.

Bošnjak, M. (2011). *Globalna finansijska i ekonomska kriza i njen uticaj na finansije i privredu Srbije, Studija za sajt Ministarstva finansija*. Retrieved March 5, 2016, from http://www.mfp.gov.rs/UserFiles/File/dokumenti/GLOBALNA%20FIN_i%20ek_kriza%20i%20njen%20uticaj%20na%20priv_Srbije_17_2_2011_.pdf

Carlin, W., Fries, S. M., Schaffer, M. E., & Seabright, P. (2001). Competition and enterprise performance in transition economies: Evidence from a cross-country survey. William Davidson Institute Working Paper No. 376. SSRN Electronic Journal.

Carree, M., & Thurik, A. R. (1998). Small firms and economic growth in Europe. *Atlantic Economic Journal, 26*(2), 137–146. https://doi.org/10.1007/BF02299356

Carree, M. A., & Thurik, A. R. (2003). The impact of entrepreneurship on economic growth. In Z. J. Acs & D. B. Audretsch (Eds.), *Handbook of entrepreneurship research* (pp. 437–471). Boston: Kluwer Academic Publishers.

Carree, M., Van Stel, A., & Thurik, R. (2005). The effect of entrepreneurial activity on national economic growth. *Small Business Economics., 24*, 311–321.

Commission of the European Communities. (2007). *Improving knowledge transfer between research institutions and industry across Europe: Embracing open innovation–Implementing the Lisbon agenda, communication from the Commission to the Council the European Parliament, the European Economic and Social Committee and the Committee of the Region*. COM 182, Brussels, 4 April 2007, Retrieved December 19, 2016, from http://ec.europa.eu/invest-in-research/pdf/com2007182_en.pdf

Čučković, N., & Bartlett, W. (2007). Entrepreneurship and competitiveness: The Europeanisation of small and medium-sized enterprise policy in Croatia. *Southeast European and Black Sea Studies, 7*(1), 37–56. https://doi.org/10.1080/14683850701189311

Filipović, S. (2003). Ograničavajući faktori razvoja MSP u Srbiji. *Industrija, 31*(3–4), 26.

Harrison, B. (1994). The small firms myth. *California Management Review, 36*(3), 142–158.

Iglesias-Sánchez, P. P., Jambrino-Maldonado, C., Velasco, A. P., & Kokash, H. (2016). Impact of entrepreneurship programmes on university students. *Education + Training, 58*(2), 209–228. https://doi.org/10.1108/ET-01-2015-0004

Ivanović-Đukić, M., & Lazić, M. (2014). Encouraging innovation of small and medium enterprises in Serbia to support competitiveness improvement in post-crisis period. *Ekonomske teme, 52*(1), 49–62.

Ivanović-Đukić, M., & Lepojević, V. (2015a). The effect of entrepreneurial activity on national competitivenes: A comparative analysis of developed and developing countries. In B. Krstić (Ed.), *Improving the efficiency and competitiveness of enterprises and national economies, International Thematic Collection of Papers* (pp. 169–191). Niš: Faculty of Economics, University of Niš.

Ivanović-Đukić, M., & Lepojević, V. (2015b). Corporate social responsibility and firm efficiency in Serbia. *Engineering Economics, 26*(5), 551–559. https://doi.org/10.5755/j01.ee.26.5.8756

Ivanović-Đukić, M., & Stefanović, S. (2011a). Analysis of business performance of entrepreneurs in Serbia with purpouse of strengthening their competitivenes. In B. Krstić (Ed.), *Improving the competitivenes of the public and private sector by networking competences, International Thematic Collection of Papers* (pp. 349–368). Niš: Faculty of Economics, University of Niš.

Ivanović-Đukić, M., & Stefanović, S. (2011b). Support to the development of entrepreneurship in the Nišava region in order to increase competitiveness and overcome economic crisis. In *Experiences in overcoming the global economic crisis–the cases of Italy and Serbia, International Thematic Collection of Papers* (pp. 187–208). Niš: Faculty of Economics, University of Niš.

Lampe, J. R. (1975). Finance and pre-1914 industrial stirrings in Bulgaria and Serbia. *Southeastern Europe, 2*(1), 23–52. https://doi.org/10.1163/187633375X00025

Lampe, J. R., & Jackson, M. R. (1982). *Balkan economic history, 1550–1950: From imperial borderlands to developing nations*. Bloomington: Indiana University Press.

McMillian, J., & Woodruff, C. (2002). The central role of entrepreneurs in transition economies. *The Journal of Economic Perspectives, 16*(3), 153–170. https://doi.org/10.1257/089533002760278767

Megginson, W., & Netter, J. (2001). From state to market: A survey of empirical studies on privatization. *Journal of Economic Literature, 39*(2), 321–339.

Mičeta, L. (2015). *Despot Stefan Lazarević. Biografija prvog Beograđanina*. Beograd: Laguna.

Mihaljčić, R. (1997). *Zakon o rudnicima despota Stefana Lazarevića*. Beograd: Enciklopedija srpske istoriografije.

Moreno, A. M., & Casillas, J. C. (2007). High-growth SMEs version non-high-growth SMEs: A discriminant analysis. *Entrepreneurship & Regional Development, 19*, 69–88.

Naudé, W. (2008). *Entrepreneurship and economic development: Theory, evidence and policy*; IZA DPNo. 7507. Retrieved July 1, 2017, from http://ftp.iza.org/dp7507.pdf

Naudé, W. (2013). *Entrepreneurship and economic development: theory, evidence and policy*; IZA DPNo.7507. Retrieved July 01, 2017, from http://ftp.iza.org/dp7507.pdf

Petković, S. (2017). University students' entrepreneurial intentions: Insights from BiH (Republic of Srpska). *Acta Economica, 15*(27), 59–92.

Salgado-Banda, H. (2007). Entrepreneurship and economic growth: An empirical analysis. *Journal of Developmental Entrepreneurship, 12*(1), 3–29. https://doi.org/10.1142/S1084946707000538

Saopštenja o poslovanju privrede u Republici Srbiji od 2004. do 2014. godine. (2015). Retrieved April 1, 2016, from http://www.apr.gov.rs/Registri/Finansijskiizveštajiibonitet/Makroekonomskasaopštenja.aspx

Schwab, K. (2014). *The global competitiveness report 2014–2015*. Retrieved March 12, 2016, from http://www3.weforum.org/docs/WEF_GlobalCompetitivenessReport_2014-15.pdf

Schumpeter, J. A. (1934). *The theory of economic development*. Cambridge: Harvard University Press.

Statistical office of the Republic Serbia. (2017). *Data. Latest indicators*. Retrieved July 21, 2017, from http://www.stat.gov.rs/WebSite/Public/PageView.aspx?pKey=2

Stefanović, S., Ivanović-Đukić, M., & Janković-Milić, V. (2013). The analysis of key challenges and constraints to the stability and growth of an entrepreneurial sector in Serbia. *Journal of Balkan and Near Eastern Studies, 15*(3), 346–365. https://doi.org/10.1080/19448953.2013.789330

Stel, A., Carree, M., & Thurik, R. (2005). The effect of entrepreneurial activity on national economic growth. *Small Business Economics, 24*, 311–321. https://doi.org/10.1007/s11187-005-1996-6

The President of Republic Serbia. (2017). *Constitution of Republic Serbia*. Retrieved July 05, 2017, from http://www.predsednik.rs/en/documents/constitution-republic-serbia

Valliere, D., & Peterson, R. (2009). Entrepreneurship and economic growth: Evidence from emerging and developed countries. *Entrepreneurship & Regional Development, 21*, 459–480. https://doi.org/10.1080/08985620802332723

Van Praag, C. M., & Versloot, P. H. (2007). What is the value of entrepreneurship? A review of recent research. *Small Business Economics, 29*(4), 351–382. https://doi.org/10.1007/s11187-007-9074-x

Vučo, N. (1955). *Privredna istorija Srbije do prvog svetskog rata*. Beograd: Naučna knjiga.

Wong, P. K., Ho, Y. P., & Autio, E. (2005). Entrepreneurship, innovation and economic growth: Evidence from GEM data. *Small Business Economics, 24*(3), 335–350. https://doi.org/10.1007/s11187-005-2000-1

World Economic Forum. (2015). *The global competitiveness report 2015–2016*. Retrieved July 28, 2017, from http://www3.weforum.org/docs/gcr/2015-2016/Global_Competitiveness_Report_2015-2016.pdf

Saša Petković, PhD, is associate professor at the Faculty of Economics of the University of Banja Luka. His subjects are entrepreneurship, economics and management of SMEs and management of entrepreneurial projects, theoretical economics and entrepreneurship scientific area. He authored or coauthored 25 published research papers in scientific journals and proceedings of the correspondent conferences and seven monographs (three in Springer Publishing). He carried out research and scientific stays in several countries: USA, UK, Brazil, Spain, Germany, Austria, Holland, Bulgaria, Slovenia, Hungary, Croatia, etc. Beside his work at the Faculty, he has been engaged in work of international development organization CARE International Balkans since 1999 as a project manager with Head of Office in Sarajevo and Branch Office in Banja Luka.

Maja Ivanović Đukić, associate professor at the Department of Management, Faculty of Economics, University of Nis, Republic of Serbia, has been an active researcher in a number of areas—Entrepreneurship and SMEs, Management strategy, Organizational behavior, and Corporate Social responsibility. As an author and coauthor, she wrote more than 100 scientific publications published in international journals as well as in the leading national journals and international conference proceedings. She has been engaged in the various national and international projects and activities in the fields of Entrepreneurship and Management.

Entrepreneurship in Slovenia

Laxman Panthi, Bostjan Antoncic, and Robert D. Hisrich

Abstract Slovenia is a country with a solid economy concentrated in industry and a stable democracy since the breakup of Yugoslavia and the entrance of the country into NATO and the EU in 2004 and the euro zone in 2007. The success of the country in terms of economic development should continue with more enterprises being privatized and an increasing number of registered incorporated firms. The location of the country provides opportunities for growth particularly in the surrounding developing countries.

1 Introduction

Slovenia (Slovene: Slovenija) is a Republic in South East Europe, the Balkan Peninsula, formerly a constituent republic of Yugoslavia. Slovenia is bounded on the North by Austria, on the North East by Hungary, on the South East and the South by Croatia, and on the West by Italy and the Adriatic Sea. Slovenia covers an area of 20,251 km^2 (land: 20,273 km^2; water: 122 km^2). Ljubljana (Exhibits 1 and 2) is the capital of Republic of Slovenia (Funk & Wagnalls New World Encyclopedia 2016).

L. Panthi
Medical Mutual of Omaha, Omaha, NE, USA
e-mail: lpanthi@kent.edu

B. Antoncic (✉)
University of Ljubljana, Ljubljana, Slovenia
e-mail: bostjan.antoncic@ef.uni-lj.si

R. D. Hisrich
Kent State University, Kent, OH, USA
e-mail: rhisric1@kent.edu

© Springer International Publishing AG, part of Springer Nature 2018   131
R. Palalić et al. (eds.), *Entrepreneurship in Former Yugoslavia*,
https://doi.org/10.1007/978-3-319-77634-7_8

Exhibit 1 Ljubljana, the capital city. © 2017 Bettina L. Hisrich

Exhibit 2 Ljubljana center by night. © 2017 Janez Tomc

1.1 Demographics

- Population: 2,063,768 (2015)
- Ethnic groups: Slovene 83.1%, Serb 2%, Croat 1.8%, Bosniak 1.1%, other or unspecified 12% (2002 census)
- Languages: Slovenian (official) 91.1%, Serbo-Croatian 4.5%, other or unspecified 4.4%, Italian (official, only in municipalities where Italian national communities reside), Hungarian (official, only in municipalities where Hungarian national communities reside) (2002 census)
- Religions: Catholic 57.8%, Muslim 2.4%, Orthodox 2.3%, other Christian 0.9%, unaffiliated 3.5%, other or unspecified 23%, no religion 10.1% (2002 census)

2 Historical Overview

The Slovene lands were part of the Austro-Hungarian Empire until they dissolute at the end of World War I. In 1918, the Slovenes joined the Serbs and Croats in forming a new multinational state, which was named Yugoslavia in 1929. After World War II, Slovenia became a republic of the renewed Yugoslavia, which though communist, distanced itself from Moscow's rule. Dissatisfied with the exercise of power by the majority Serbs, the Slovenes succeeded in establishing their independence in 1991 after a short 10-day war.

Historical ties to Western Europe, a strong economy, and a stable democracy have assisted in Slovenia's transformation to a modern state. Slovenia acceded to both NATO and the EU in the spring of 2004; it joined the euro zone in 2007. Slovenia, and Lake Bled, was the summer home of the former Yugoslavian emperor, Tito (Exhibit 3). The flag of Slovenia features three equal horizontal bands of white,

Exhibit 3 Lake Bled, Tito's summer capital. © 2017 Janez Tomc

Exhibit 4 The flag of Slovenia

blue, and red, with Slovenian coat of arms included between the white and blue bands (Exhibit 4).

3 Environment for Entrepreneurship

3.1 *Economy*

The World Bank reported the Slovenia's GDP (current US$) to be 43.072 billion and the per capita (current US$) to be 20,873 in 2015 (World Bank Data 2016). Exhibit 5 shows its comparison of GDP growth rate from the 1991 to 2014.

Although Slovenia only accounted for the 8% of the total area of the former Yugoslavia, their economy was the most developed in terms of industry and other production. Slovenia is a member of the OECD and European Union. In the first year of independence, Slovenia faced numerous problems in the economy: the industrial production fell by 24% and the agricultural sector was the only sector to have at least 0% change (Zizmond 1993). The entire 1990s, Slovenia went through several reforms in political and economic policies in lieu of transformation to a market-based as well as a national economy. Slovenia responded with a rapid GDP growth rate even more than the EU periphery in the first year of independence. (Svetlicic and Rojec 1998). However, it has grown to be one of the strongest countries economically in the former East Europe.

The Slovene economy is heavily concentrated in industry as opposed to the fellow OECD members. The Slovenian economy is similar to other Eastern European economies in many ways: very small privately owned sector and full employment with substantial excess demand for labor and a well-educated labor force.

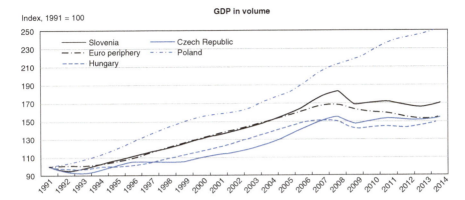

Index, 1991 = 100

GDP in volume

Exhibit 5 GDP in volume comparison with similar countries. Source: OECD Economic Outlook Database

3.2 Entrepreneurship and SMEs Sector

A historical perspective on small and medium enterprises in Slovenia can be described as follows (Glas et al. 1999: 108): "Following World War II, social ownership of business assets dominated the enterprise sector with private ownership of physical resources limited to the crafts sector, agriculture and some independent professions. In the socially owned sector, there was a lack of small firms with only a few small firms networked in subcontracting relationships with larger companies. These firms did not develop direct links to foreign markets, so any exports were indirect as parts/components of the final products marketed by the large companies. Even many larger companies entered international markets through specialized government foreign trading companies."

The structure of the economy of the former Yugoslavia (and Slovenia) was distorted and exhibited a lack of small-sized enterprises—a clear socialist black hole (Vahcic and Petrin 1989). Entry of new firms and breaking up existing firms into smaller units able to compete on the market—the two key forms of new enterprise formation—were recognized to be the key vehicles that would change (and actually changed) the structure and performed the transition from a highly concentrated and inefficient market structure to a competitive market structure in former Yugoslavia and other socialist countries.

The structure of the Slovenian economy changed: "With the introduction of new Enterprise law in 1988, the economic structure changed significantly. Private ownership of firms was allowed and there was a great deal of new firm creation. The number of registered incorporated firms increased from 2500 to over 23,000 in 3 years with 52,000 being in existence at the end of 1996. The number of sole proprietors increased from 35,000 at the beginning of 1990s to nearly 60,000 at the end of 1997. As the first step of deregulation of the economy in the former Yugoslavia, the foreign trade was liberalized encouraging a vast number of import-oriented small businesses. However, due to the process of dissolution of former Yugoslavia, with Slovenia becoming a formally independent state at the end of 1991 and with the economic crises beginning in most of the transition economies, Slovenian companies lost significant markets in parts of former Yugoslavia as well as in other former COMECON countries; companies responded to this loss by: (1) increasing sales to the Slovenian market under increased competition due to the liberalized foreign trade; (2) expanding sales to European markets, partly through increased subcontracting; (3) diversifying into new business fields; and (4) decreasing the volume of production and employment. These companies were facing a difficult situation in part because they lacked experience in dealing with foreign markets. Those firms that entered foreign markets successfully discovered that the market prices in Western European markets were considerably lower than in the markets previously served. Some firms had problems adapting their products to different standards, particularly the standard of the European Union (EU)." (Glas et al. 1999: 108).

According to Antoncic and Hisrich (2003: 211–212), Slovenia, comparing to other transition economies, has been considered "a success story in terms of economic development; the country has chosen a suboptimal privatization method, which resulted in ownership structures with substantial state involvement that inhibit faster development of corporate entrepreneurship activities and are not beneficial for organizational growth and profitability. Because of a high proportion of enterprises that have undergone privatization through the redistributive privatization process in the economy, Slovenia is probably achieving suboptimal levels of GDP growth and wealth creation. Countries that went through transition from the controlled to the market-oriented economy seem to share a common characteristic of making politically acceptable privatization decisions (Wiseman 1991) at the expense of economic performance."

Antoncic and Hisrich (2003: 213) demonstrated on data from Slovenian enterprises "the privatization method that results in a higher share of private ownership makes a difference in organizational growth and profitability, particularly in terms of its strong direct effects, as well as in the mediation of corporate entrepreneurship activities that include new venture formation, product/service innovation, and process innovation. In addition, privatization time tends to be a strong predictor of subsequent organizational profitability."

The number of registered incorporated firms increased further from the end of the 1990s but at a lesser pace than in the early 1990s, as indicated by the data from the Slovenian Statistical Office (SURS 2015; number in 2014: total: 186,433; 100,356 physical persons, from which 88,528 sole proprietors and 11,828 other physical persons; 86,077 legal entities, from which 59,856 business companies and 26.221 other legal entities), despite the economic recession the number of total entities increased by 22.2% in the 2008–2014 period, with the predominance of the SME sector (absolute number: 186,103; relative number: 98.8%; number of employees: 572,049; share of GDP: 54.7%). The Global Entrepreneurship Monitor (GEM) for Slovenia (Rebernik et al. 2016) classified Slovenia in 2015 among innovation-driven economies (population: 2.1 million; GDP: USD42.8 billion; GDP Per Capita: USD20,733; the contribution of SMEs to GDP: 63%; a relatively low total early-stage entrepreneurial activity rate of 8%).

Despite the suboptimal privatization and other suboptimal economic decisions driven or supported by the politics (e.g., many financial supports for failing large companies, nationalization of some key banks with disregard of the private ownership, failed management buyouts, and company mismanagement), the Slovenian economy remained relatively stable because of its export and international orientation and the gaining and finally the prevailing role of family businesses.

Most companies in Slovenia (up to 83%) in 2014 were family run and predominantly small, with fewer than 50 employees. These family businesses generated average annual revenues of up to around 4 million Dollars individually, operated for more than 20 years, and were under the leadership of the first or second generation of owners (Antoncic et al. 2015: 4). Family businesses had a significant contribution to the Slovenian economy (Antoncic et al. 2015: 22; a contribution based on 2014 data: 69% of total sales, 67% of added value, and 70% of employment). Key factors that contributed to the success of family businesses in Slovenia were identified as follows (Antoncic et al. 2015: 24): (1) high quality products and services; (2) controlling costs; (3) established trademark and loyalty; (4) adaptable and focused leadership; and (5) long-term perspective of governance.

3.3   Port of Koper

Port of Koper (Exhibit 6) is one of the several ports located in the Adriatic Sea and a member of North Adriatic Port Association along with Rijeka, Trieste, and Venice. Port of Koper plays an important role in the economy of Slovenia. Koper

Exhibit 6 Port of Koper. © 2017 Ana Gamulin

Exhibit 7 Piran. © 2017 Janez Tomc

Exhibit 8 Piran Sea. © 2017 Janez Tomc

serves as a hub of Europe because of the two biggest highways crossing through Slovenia. Well-known places in Slovenia are Piran (Exhibits 7 and 8) and Bled (Exhibit 9) as well.

Exhibit 9 Bled Mountains. © 2017 Janez Tomc

4 Toward the Future

The future of Slovenia appears bright in terms of creating and managing an entrepreneurial firm in the economy. The economy of the country itself will ebb and flow based in part on the economies in other countries in the European Union (EU) particularly since Slovenia has changed its currency to the euro. This change of course significantly increased the cost of goods and services in the country, particularly services such as hotel rates and restaurant costs.

The geographic location of Slovenia allows entrepreneurs to grow their ventures in surrounding countries and in developing countries, for example, Serbia, Bosnia and Herzegovina, Bulgaria, Romania, Turkey, and Ukraine, as well in Russia with the established relationship. The university training in entrepreneurship remains at a high level, particularly at the University of Ljubljana. There is some capital in the county to form and grow ventures as well as incubator facilities available.

5 Case Study: Intervela D.O.O. Koper—Victory Sailmakers[1]

Zvonko Bezic and Zeljko Perovic-Huck came to know each other in the early 1970s when they both started sailing with the Galeb Sailing Club in Rijeka, Croatia. When acting as a sailing coach in Galeb, Zeljko Perovic occasionally worked with Mr. Grego, who was making sails. In 1988, Zvonko Bezic and Zeljko Perovic started

---

[1]Prepared by Bostjan Antoncic, Faculty of Economics at the University in Ljubljana, Slovenia.

to make sails on their own, at first only for the smallest Optimist-class sailboats. Later they started to manufacture sails for larger sailboats and yachts. Initially, they cut the material for sails in the school gym they hired on weekends, and on weekdays they sewed them at home together with Zeljko Perovic's grandmother. In 1990, they decided to go into the sail business full time. All management tasks have been in the hands of the owners: Zvonko Bezic primarily responsible for marketing and Zeljko Perovic for production.

Zvonko Bezic and Zeljko Perovic were involved in competitive sailing activities from their early days. However, they did not have any business experience at the time of start-up. They have overcome this weakness and start-up problems with persistence that may in part come from their passion for sailing.

The market for sails in Croatia and Slovenia drastically shrank in 1991, so they stopped manufacturing sails and only maintained some resale business and decided to move to Koper, Slovenia, where they rented premises in the Koper Marina. At the beginning of 1992, they started to use computer technology for design and production of their sails.

The marketing strategy formulation in 1993 has been an important turning point toward growth. Growth was set as a primary goal. They have also set their goals for a gradual increase in market share, the promotion of the company and its products to potential customers, and an improvement in the internal efficiency of the company and the quality of its products. The strengths (price and quality, including the finishing of sails and a 2-year warranty), weaknesses (marketing communication, standardization, design), opportunities (selling larger series to companies, manufacturing sails for larger yachts), and threats (market contraction, poor advertising for sails, and essential technological changes) were established for sails—the key product of the company. Development and market penetration were made the primary focus of the company's business plan. In line with such, the marketing strategy was formulated by the elements of the marketing mix: product (standardization, design improvements, the transfer of improvements from racing sails to other sails, following trends closely, the introduction and improvement of after-sale services—i.e., the tuning of sails and instructing customers, as well as research and development—mainly into the use of new materials), price (competitive prices and price discrimination with regard to individual customers), place (the extension of the distribution network), and promotion (promotion by means of a first-class sailboat—Gaia Cube—in races, personal contacts established at races, the mailing and distribution of promotional material to sailboat owners, and advertising in the Slovenian nautical magazine "Val"). They focused on the promotion of the Victory sail trademark. They have succeeded to execute most of the plan.

Following this strategy and with innovations, the owners grew their firm, with revenues of over 100,000 Dollars in 1995 and over 500,000 Dollars in 1999. Some most important events in the 1995–2001 period:

- The purchase of a cutter in 1995.
- The acquisition of the Kutin sail loft and start of parallel production in Rijeka.
- Sail production for the sailboat producer Elan.

- Participation in the Gaia Cube project.
- Penetration of the global market with Finn class sails.
- Start of production of sails for Europe, Optimist, and 470 class.
- Start a more formalized promotion and advertising in 2000 and 2001.
- Outsourcing and reorganization.

In 2001, they made expansion plans and found themselves in front of three alternative future choices:

- Take a foreign trade name and work as a member of a group.
- Merge with foreign companies, concerning which negotiations were already underway.
- Sell the company—find a potential partner with money who would acquire a part of or their entire company.

With the actual prospects of Slovenia joining the European Union in 2004, they decided to purchase a bankrupt textile plant in the Slovenian town of Materija and moved there in 2003. They financed their new plant through excess cash flows and a bank loan. The international expansion was well set and begun to bear fruit in the 2004–2006 period. However, a tragedy struck on the July 6, 2006, at 6 pm; Zvonko Bezic passed away in an accident with his new motorbike on a road in Istria. Zeljko Perovic decided to join ONE Sails network as an independent partner in order to strengthen the marketing efforts. The company further improved the market position until 2008 with growth in revenues to 2.6 million Dollars. During the crisis, the company retained in a good shape but the revenues had fallen to 1.4 million Dollars by 2010 and soon partially recuperated to 1.8 million Dollars in 2011 and 2012, with 1.5 million Dollars in 2013, 1.9 million Dollars in 2014, and 1.7 million Dollars in 2015.

References

Antoncic, B., Auer Antoncic, J., & Juricic, D. (2015). *Family business characteristics in Slovenia.* Ljubljana: Ernst & Young.
Antoncic, B., & Hisrich, R. D. (2003). Privatization, corporate entrepreneurship, and performance: Testing a normative model. *Journal of Developmental Entrepreneurship, 8*(3), 197–218.
Funk & Wagnalls New World Encyclopedia. (2016). *Slovenia data.* Retrieved March 10, 2017, from data.worldbank.org
Glas, M., Hisrich, R. D., Vahcic, A., & Antoncic, B. (1999). The internationalization of SMEs in transition economies: Evidence from Slovenia. *Global Focus, 11*(4), 107–124.
Rebernik, M., Crnogaj, K., & Hojnik, B. (2016). *Podjetnistvo med priloznostjo in nujo: GEM Slovenija 2015.* Maribor: Ekonomsko-poslovna fakulteta.
SURS. (2015). *Statisticni urad Republike Slovenije, Novonastala podjetja.* Ljubljana: Statisticni urad Republike Slovenije.
Svetlicic, M., & Rojec, M. (1998). Short overview of the Slovenian economy and foreign investment in Slovenia. *Eastern European Economics, 36*(5), 60–72.
Vahcic, A., & Petrin, T. (1989). Financial system for restructuring the Yugoslav economy. In C. Kessides, T. King, M. Nuti, & C. Sokil (Eds.), *Financial reform in socialist economies*

(pp. 154–161). Washington, DC/Florence: Economic Development Institute of the World Bank/ The European University Institute.

Wiseman, J. (1991). Privatization in the command economy. In A. F. Ott & K. Hartley (Eds.), *Privatization and economic efficiency: A comparative analysis of developed and developing countries* (pp. 257–270). Aldershot: Edward Elgar.

World Bank Data. (2016). *Country profile: Slovenia*. Retrieved from https://data.worldbank.org/country/slovenia

Zizmond, E. (1993). Slovenia – One year of independence. *Europe-Asia Studies, 45*(5), 887–905.

Laxman Panthi is a Data Warehouse Developer at Medical Mutual of Ohio, USA. He completed his Master's in Business Administration from Kent State University, USA. His area of expertise are data analysis & visualization and his research interest is primarily in emerging markets, regional development, international entrepreneurship, and business innovation. He has worked on papers on business innovation, bee entrepreneurship, and regional development.

Bostjan Antoncic, Ph.D., is Professor of Entrepreneurship at the Faculty of Economics, University of Ljubljana. His areas of expertise include corporate entrepreneurship, entrepreneurial networks, entrepreneurial personality, and international entrepreneurship. He has written several books—more than ten in the area of entrepreneurship alone, as well as several business research articles. The titles of the books were, for example, *Entrepreneurship* (2002, 2008), *Entrepreneurship Cases – Growth and Development* (2002), *Entrepreneurship Cases – Start-Up, Momentum and Growth* (2005), *The Personal Resource-Acquisition Network of the Entrepreneur and Small Firm Growth* (2007), *Business Plan Preparation Guidebook* (2008), and *Entrepreneurship Cases – Founding and Management of Firms* (2013). His papers have been published in academic journals such as the *Journal of Business Venturing, Entrepreneurship and Regional Development, Industrial Management & Data Systems, Technovation, Transformations in Business & Economics, Journal of Business Economics and Management,* and *Journal of Small Business Management.*

Robert D. Hisrich is the Bridgestone Chair of International Marketing and Associate Dean of Graduate and International Programs at the College of Business Administration at Kent State University. He holds a B.A. from DePauw University and an M.B.A. and a doctorate from the University of Cincinnati. Professor Hisrich's research pursuits are focused on entrepreneurship and venture creation: entrepreneurial ethics, corporate entrepreneurship, women and minority entrepreneurs, venture financing, and global venture creation. He teaches courses and seminars in these areas, as well as in marketing management, and product planning and development. His interest in global management and entrepreneurship resulted in two Fulbright Fellowships in Budapest, Hungary, honorary degrees from Chuvash State University (Russia) and University of Miskolc (Hungary), and being a visiting faculty member in universities in Austria, Australia, Ireland, and Slovenia. Professor Hisrich serves on the editorial boards of several prominent journals in entrepreneurial scholarship, is on several boards of directors, and is author or coauthor of over 300 research articles appearing in journals such as *Journal of Marketing, Journal of Marketing Research, Journal of Business Venturing, Journal of Developmental Entrepreneurship, and Entrepreneurship Theory and Practice.* Professor Hisrich has authored, coauthored, or edited 46 books or their editions, including: *Marketing* (2000, 2nd ed.)*; How to Fix and Prevent the 13 Biggest Problems That Derail Business* (2004)*; Technology Entrepreneurship* (2015, 2nd ed.)*; Entrepreneurial Finance* (2015); *International Entrepreneurship* (2016, 3rd ed.); *Advanced Introduction to Corporate Venturing* (2016); *Effective Entrepreneurial Management* (2017); and *Entrepreneurship* (2017, 10th ed.)*.*

Entrepreneurship in Former Yugoslavia: Toward the Future

Ramo Palalić, Léo Paul Dana, and Veland Ramadani

Abstract This chapter summarizes the ex-Yugoslavia region in terms of its historical events, entrepreneurship development, and state of economy of Yugoslavia. Moreover, it reviews each of ex-Yugoslavia republics. Also, it revises each country's profile regarding entrepreneurship and business environment. Additionally, it discusses challenges and perspectives of each country.

1 Introduction

Tito's Yugoslavia lasted 45 years and his leadership passed through severe stages until *his* Yugoslavia was established. In the early stages after World War II, Yugoslavia was destroyed, and the country became very poor and hungry. During the late 1940s, Yugoslavia was in its worse state until its dissolution. Besides a bad internal situation, in which the whole country and infrastructure were destroyed, foreign politics were also not good. Yugoslavia was kicked out from the East Block led by former Union of Soviet Socialist Republics (USSR); relationship with Italy and Austria on the west, Hungary on north, and Albania and Greece on the southeast was terrible. Simply, Yugoslavia was on its own. The government had devoted its full energy to rebuilding the country in every sphere and cleanse the country from those who supported the East Block politics (*InfoBiro*[1]). However, Tito started to connect with the Western Europe through the Scandinavian countries in the early

---

[1]For more info, see Rubinstain (1970), Rossidis (2009).

R. Palalić (✉)
International University of Sarajevo, Sarajevo, Bosnia and Herzegovina
e-mail: rpalalic@ius.edu.ba

L. P. Dana
Montpellier Business School, Montpellier, France
e-mail: lp.dana@supco-montpellier.fr

V. Ramadani
South-East European University, Tetovo, Macedonia
e-mail: v.ramadani@seeu.edu.mk

© Springer International Publishing AG, part of Springer Nature 2018
R. Palalić et al. (eds.), *Entrepreneurship in Former Yugoslavia*,
https://doi.org/10.1007/978-3-319-77634-7_9

1950s, and his first visit to Western Europe was to the UK. Then normalization of relationships between the Western Europe and the USA started, as well as with neighboring countries.

The model of diversity in this region was under the control of Tito's regime. The diversity, brotherhood, and unity (*bratstvo i jedinstvo*[2]) have been promoted across the whole Yugoslavia and in overall, everyone at that time accepted this model. So the "Yugopluralist model" earlier discussed by Ramadani and Dana (2013) functioned under the specific circumstances and constraints. When this model was not supported by Croatia and Slovenia, due to overcontrol of Serbia, then the dissolution of Yugoslavia was gradually announced. As outcomes of those disputes, the war happened (aggression to Croatia and Bosnia and Herzegovina) and lasted 5 years.

The model of the economy was something in between the Russian model and free-market one. However, it prevailed more to Russian with certain differences in it. Capitalism, on the other side, was known among people as a horrible pattern of the economy in which employees do not have rights they deserve. Ordinary people believed that *labor self-governance* (*radnicko samoupravljanje*) is the best what could happen to all employees across Yugoslavia.

Entrepreneurial activities were reduced to a minimum to some small artisans who possessed their business premises in crowded places. Public or government support of those activities was actively discouraged. One of the reasons is that if capitalism will take place, many people claimed that they would be jobless and the job distribution, as well as social welfare, will not be just. This economic model, the command economy, was accepted widely and people of Yugoslavia were relying on this model as the one which does not have an alternative. What, when, where, and how much will be produced was decided by the centralized Government in Belgrade. Law of supply and demand was monitored by the government, and not by the market, which had discretional right on any decision related to this Law. Import was reduced to a minimum, to only goods that are necessary. Export was done through the countries who were members of the "non-alignment movement" led by Tito, Nasser (Egypt), and Nehru (India).

The non-aligned movement was established in Brijuni, Croatia, on 18–19 July 1956 (Bilandžić 1978, p. 220). This movement was established as a reflection of two blocks which had different political and economic views. Establishment of this movement for Yugoslavia was very palmy. Economic exchange with core countries of this movement was tremendous. For instance, within 10 years, the exchange increased enormously. The exchange with India was from 7.8 million to 6.5 billion of Ruplja. Moreover, Yugoslavia helped other non-aligned movement countries in their development by providing loans for their infrastructure and industry development and advancements. When it comes to the decision making of these non-align movement countries, Yugoslavia was the critical and influential decision maker

---

[2]*Bratstvo I jedinstvo* was a powerful slogan to keep people attached to each other and it united all peoples of Yugoslavia regardless of race, gender, nation and religion.

among other alliance members (Petković 1983). The leadership of this movement Yugoslavia made very strong and respected in the world.

Prior to the crisis of the 1980s, Yugoslavia was one among the world's thriving countries, achieving outstanding results in development results; for instance, with an average growth rate of 6.1% of GDP it was one of the fastest industrial growth in the world. There was a narrow range in development between Yugoslavia and developed countries. In 1952, this ratio was 1:10.5, in 1959 1:6, in 1965 1:5.1, and in 1970 1:4.4. In the early 1950s, Yugoslavia's income per capita was half of what was the world average and in 1978 was about 20% higher (from the world average). Industrial production in 1977 was 14 times higher than in 1947. Agricultural yields per hectare were twice as large as before the war and were among the largest in the world (Bilandžić 1978, p. 462).

This was the state left after Tito's death. Problems occurred along the following decade. The deficit has grown up to USD7.5 billion. Inflation rate started to grow to 45% annually, and unemployment rate started to increase by over 27% in Kosovo. A mass phenomenon of nationalism appeared. Some ethnic groups realized that the power was not equally distributed along human, political, and economic spheres. This has fired up national leaders to take an opportunity to separate from Yugoslavia and to be stand-alone states.

As mentioned above, wars from 1991 to 1995 and in Kosovo from February 1998 until June 1999 have created a new economic region. Cultural values are overlapping to some extend while all republics can speak Serbo-Croatian (*Srpsko-Hrvatski jezik*).

2   Toward the Future

Currently, from former Yugoslavia, there are six independent countries along with Kosovo (for which negotiations are in process). All of them have own independent political and economic system.

Bosnia and Herzegovina, the heart of ex-Yugoslavia, were among best Yugoslavian Republics (Palalic et al. 2017). During that time it had an excellent infrastructure, and it was known for successful global brands (Famos, Energoinvest, Unis, Pretis, BNT Novi Travnik, etc.) which were based on intensive industry. Since its inception, in 1992, the country passed through a very difficult time from 1992 to 1995. Besides war challenges, now it faces with dysfunctional political structure, which consumes a lot of resources and capital. An extensive public administration, outdated laws from Tito's Yugoslavia, prevents the development of entrepreneurship. Many beaurocracy and taxation procedures led to the prolonged development of new startups and new ventures. Doing business in Bosnia is lastly favored place among ex-Yugoslavia's republics, 86th (Doing Business 2017). However, the state strives to make progress regarding socioeconomic development which will support entrepreneurship development in the long term. Negotiations for accession to the EU already started, and in December 2016 B&H has received the European Commission's Questionnaire for the accession of B&H into EU. Additionally, along this,

Bosnia has adopted a Reform Agenda to adapt to EU business environment. Reform Agenda for Bosnia and Herzegovina scheduled 2015–2018 consists of six areas: public finance, taxation and fiscal sustainability; the business climate and competitiveness: the labour market; social welfare and pension reform; the rule of law and good governance; and public administration reform. Hopefully, it will succeed by the end of 2018, which will open a newly designed gate for entrepreneurship. Apart from this, Bosnia has been placed as the third highest tourism growth rate globally between 1995 and 2020 (World population review 2017). Tourism in Bosnia is flourishing but still drain down by rigid government's business policies. As Croatia, Bosnia suffers from a decrease in population. Migration to other countries is trendy while the State does not do much regarding this very serious issue. The country of Bosnia and Herzegovina has the natural potential to be one of the prominent Balkan countries in entrepreneurial activities, intensive industry, energy sector, and tourism. Now, it is Bosnian Government's call.

Croatia was the second republic in Yugoslavia which got independence in 1991. However, compared to Slovenia, which had only 2 weeks of the war, Croatia had war challenges from 1991 to 1995. Half of the country was destroyed and that had slowed down the country's development. Doing business in Croatia is far behind Slovenia. According to World Bank's most recent annual World Bank (SB) report (Doing Business 2017) on Doing Business, it has ranked Croatia at a 51st place among the 190 countries in the world and puts down Croatia eight points from last year's placement. There are areas in which the country should improve to align with EU standards of doing business. The country deals with population issues, corruption and transparency, and nationalism, which make obstacles to entrepreneurship development. According to the World Population Review (2017):

> Croatia is in demographic crisis and losing people each year. Its fertility rate is just 1.5 children per woman, one of the world's lowest, and its death rate has exceeded the birth rate since 1991. Natural growth is negative. Croatia is now ranked as the 14th fastest shrinking country in the world. It is predicted that Croatia's population will shrink to 3.1 million by 2050, after reaching its peak of 4.7 million in 1991.

This is important because population makes the market from which every buyer and/or seller will benefit. If this trend continues, entrepreneurship development will be losing its direction.

Croatia has its potentials as well. Geostrategic position in the Adriatic Sea makes the country much known in the world. Croatia has one of the beautiful seasides, which contributes to tourism, which is one of the sectors that creates many values for Croatia's economy. The country also has the infrastructure and fertile soil that can be a reasonable basis for foreign investors and small business startups (agriculture). In overall, Croatia has entrepreneurial potentials if the state will cherish it and wisely use it in the future.

Kosovo has recorded a positive population growth. Compared to the rest of ex-Yugoslavia republics, Kosovo has the biggest density. The population is quite young which is promising for the future generation. The country is rich in natural resources, and it used to be an agro-cultural republic. Current political issues produce obstacles to entrepreneurship development. However, according to Doing Business (2017), Kosovo takes its 40th place. Additionally, Kosovo has established *Innovation Center of Kosovo (ICK)* whose purpose is to create an environment which will produce more jobs across the whole country. Kosovo, like other republics of Ex-Yugoslavia, streams toward EU membership which will find its place in the big family, the EU.

Macedonia is the best performer in terms of doing business efficiently. It takes 11th place in the global ranking (Doing Business 2017). This shows that Macedonia opened the door for FDI and set the environment positive toward entrepreneurship development. The country has natural potential for its development. Macedonian EU membership will help local entrepreneurs to finance their startups and new ventures. The government needs to support entrepreneurial activities which will be reflected in innovative products which will be pillars of the country's foreign exchange. This will boost the GDP level. Additionally, business incubation is necessary. As the chief in charge, the government should play a role, in reality, in allowing business flows to grow smoothly. A current political climate with neighbors makes these things more difficult to implement. As one of the best ex-Yugoslavian republics regarding doing business at the global ranking, Macedonia has bright perspective. Wise strategic moves of government will make Macedonia very prosperous and favorable for FDI and entrepreneurs, which will be reflected in the socioeconomic development of the country.

Montenegro is the smallest country established in the region of ex-Yugoslavia, with a population over 600,000. Entrepreneurship in this country started to grow. The state also realizes after almost two decades that job creation depends on entrepreneurship in the country and intensity how much it is supported by the government. The geographical position of the country makes it open to international countries as well as to ex-Yugoslavia region. Tourism, due to unstable political situation in specific regions, moved to this region and Montenegro became one of favorite destinations in the Europe and world. However, migration of people to other countries makes difficult for Montenegro to rely on its own skilled labor and experts. It used to be very well equipped in every sector of industry; however, it now demands skilled people from other countries in the region and the world. As Bosnia and Serbia, Montenegro is also one of potential EU members. It is already in NATO, which benefits the country regarding regional stability. Montenegro is rich with natural resources and tourism potentials. Doing business (2017) placed Montenegro at 42nd, one place ahead of Serbia. The future is dependent on the State strategy toward entrepreneurship, which hopefully will place Montenegro among favorable destinations to live.

Serbia is the biggest ex-Yugoslav republic in terms of land and population (over 8 million). Facing challenges from the war in the 1990s, Serbia is trying to be an EU member. It made progress regarding preparing the environment for favorable entrepreneurship landscape. Negotiations with the EU are in progress. Doing business placed Serbia at 43rd place, among 190 countries. It is behind Montenegro, Slovenia, and Macedonia, but ahead Croatia, Kosovo, and Bosnia. The political situation in Serbia represents a *buffer,* which sometimes works as positive and sometimes as harmful toward entrepreneurship development. SMEs are facing similar problems like in other ex-Yugoslavia republics (except Slovenia) regarding taxes and other business policies. Serbia is not isolated from declining number of population. When it comes to population rate, World Review Population (2017) summarizes about Serbia's current demography:

> Serbia has been struggling to overcome its population decline, even turning to singles nights, generous maternity leave and cash bonuses for new parents in some towns. Despite its best efforts, Serbia has been unable to reverse this trend, and its population is expected to continue its downward movement for many years.

The country has to do a lot more regarding the fertile business environment and support innovative entrepreneurial activities across the country. Once it becomes EU member, it will be more comfortable doing business, and hopefully, the business environment will be positively changed.

Slovenia was the first to get independence from ex-Yugoslavia in 1991. As one of its republics, Slovenia was the most developed republic at that time. The country has a geostrategic position that connects it with the West Europe and to the rest of Balkan countries. Informally, Slovenia was never considered as one of the Balkan countries due to its geographical location. After its independence from Yugoslavia, Slovenia has developed a lot regarding private ownership and family businesses. The state has regulated on time laws that will encourage small business which constitutes one-third of Slovenian economic and sales values. The employment rate is lowest compared to ex-Yugoslavia republics. It has intensive industry, and their products compete with European ones easily. The country possesses skilled labor force, and it has excess in labor demand. The market of Slovenia is not significant; however, its products are sold across the whole Europe including ex-Yugoslavia region. Moreover, presence in global markets like the Middle East and Gulf region makes the country's economy stronger and open to its development and advancements. Out of 190 countries in the world monitored by the World Bank (Doing business), in this year Slovenia takes 37th place (Doing Business 2017).

The region of ex-Yugoslavia is fascinating due to its geostrategic position, religious, cultural, and ethnic diversity. It cannot be cast out from the Europe geographically, and socioeconomic development is not satisfactory to join the EU. Intensive negotiations are taking place for Bosnia, Serbia, Macedonia, Montenegro, and Kosovo. The future will prevail in their EU membership.

Each independent country in this region has positive and negative circumstances. Negative ones are created by the war in the 1990s, while others are naturally positive. Positive ones are regarding the geographical position, natural resources wealth, tourism perspective, and cheap labor force. Except for Slovenia, all of them are still under war impression. However, as EU negotiation process will progress, a favorable entrepreneurial environment will be created. It needs some more time, but the dream will come true, for sure.

References

Bilandžić, D. (1978). *Historija Socijalisticke Federativne Jugoslavije: glavni procesi: 1918–1985*. Zagreb: Školska knjiga.

Doing Business. (2017). Accessed December 7, 2017, from http://www.doingbusiness.org/reports/global-reports/doing-business-2017

Palalic, R., Ramadani, V., & Dana, L. P. (2017). Entrepreneurship in Bosnia and Herzegovina: Focus on gender. *European Business Review, 29*(4), 476–496.

Petković, R. (1983). Spoljna pilitika Jugoslavije. *Politička Misao, 20*(4), 29–37.

Ramadani, V., & Dana, L.-P. (2013). The state of entrepreneurship in the Balkans: Evidence from selected countries. In V. Ramadani & R. Schneider (Eds.), *Entrepreneurship in the Balkans* (pp. 217–250). Heidelberg: Springer.

Rossidis, Z. (2009). Raskid Tito-Staljin prema viđenju grčkog tiska 1948.godine. *Časopis za suvremenu povijest, 41*(2), 367–390.

Rubinstein, A. Z. (1970). *Yugoslavia and the nonaligned world*. Princeton, NJ: Princeton University Press.

Worldometers: World View Population. (2017). Retrieved December 8, 2017, from http://worldpopulationreview.com/countries/croatia-population/

Ramo Palalić is an Assistant Professor at the Management Program, Faculty of Business and Administration, International University of Sarajevo, Sarajevo, Bosnia and Herzegovina. His research interests are entrepreneurship, leadership, marketing, and management. He teaches at both undergraduate and postgraduate levels in the above areas. Apart from this, he is actively involved in business projects in the areas of entrepreneurial leadership and marketing management, in private and public organizations. He has authored and coauthored several articles in the reputable international journals. Currently, he is serving as reviewer/editor board member of a few journals.

Léo-Paul Dana earned BA and MBA degrees at McGill University and a PhD from HEC-Montreal. He is Professor of Entrepreneurship at Montpellier Business School and a member of the Entrepreneurship & Innovation chair of LabEx Entrepreneurship (University of Montpellier, France). He formerly served as Visiting Professor of Entrepreneurship at INSEAD and Deputy Director of the International Business MBA Programme at Nanyang Business School. He has published extensively in a variety of leading journals including the *British Food Journal, Cornell Quarterly, Entrepreneurship and Regional Development, Entrepreneurship: Theory and Practice, Journal of Small Business Management, Journal of World Business,* and *Small Business Economics*. His research interests focus on cultural issues, including the internationalization of entrepreneurship.

Veland Ramadani is an Associate Professor at South-East European University, Republic of Macedonia where he teaches both undergraduate and postgraduate courses in entrepreneurship and small business management. His research interests include entrepreneurship, small business management, family businesses, and venture capital investments. He authored or coauthored around eighty research articles and seventeen books. Dr. Ramadani is an Associate Editor of *International Journal of Entrepreneurship and Small Business (IJESB)*. Dr. Ramadani received the Award for Excellence 2015—Outstanding Reviewer by Emerald Group Publishing (*Journal of Enterprising Communities: People and Places in the Global Economy*).

CPSIA information can be obtained
at www.ICGtesting.com
Printed in the USA
LVHW02*1405220718
584565LV00001B/22/P